HOW THE MOTOR BUS

CAME TO

SLOUGH, WINDSOR

AND DISTRICT

1904 - 1914

****

WRITTEN AND PUBLISHED
BY
MICHAEL MILLS

Front cover picture: London General bus arriving at the Windsor terminus of service 62 from Hounslow, having come through Slough and Eton - July 1912.

ACKNOWLEDGEMENTS

I acknowledge with gratitude the agreement of the following for the reproduction of the documents listed below:

1)　Newspaper extracts and other references:

Windsor, Eton & Slough Express ("Windsor Express")
Slough, Eton & Windsor Observer ("Slough Observer")
Slough Chronicle
Windsor Chronicle
Maidenhead Express
Bucks Free Press.

2)　Photographs (numbered illustrations):

London's Transport Museum	Front cover, 35, 36
J.M. Cummings	3, 6, 11, 12, 13, 16, 26, 28, 30, 41
Mrs J Tipping	10, 14
Slough Museum	15, 18
West Wycombe Park	23.

3)　Other Illustrations:

Slough Museum - Extracts from Headington & Sons June 1911 timetable.

Corporation of London Burnham Beeches Office - Advertisement from 1912/13 Guidebook to the Beeches.

I also acknowledge the help and encouragement of Slough Central Reference Library and the provision by the National Motor Museum of data relating to licensed vehicles.

Michael Mills

Firtrees,
Barn Close,
Farnham Common,
Slough, SL2 3JB

ISBN 0-9539609-0-0

CHAPTER 1

This book is an attempt to recount the early history of motor bus operation in and around the Slough and Windsor area and to touch on the impact which it had on the various communities. It is written very largely from the perspective of the local newspapers of the day, supplemented by facts and information from other sources and by occasional anecdotes. Having said it covers motor bus developments, it also strays into horse bus operations and into tramway and light railway proposals, as and when they arise in the chronology.

Horse bus services were still very much a feature of the local transport scene in the early 1900's, but they were seldom mentioned in the local papers. On the other hand, the relatively exciting motor bus developments were the subject of regular reporting and comment, not all of it complimentary. In the area we are looking at, as a matter of fact, tramway schemes actually constituted the first serious proposals for mechanised passenger road transport services, but with one exception, just outside the area, they all turned out to be abortive. However, the story of how trams almost came to pass right through the middle of Slough is fascinating and needs to be put on record.

As early as 1898, the London United Tramways Company, known as the LUT, had secured powers under the Light Railways Act to run electric trams as far out of London as Uxbridge. This proposal proved to be the one and only tram service which in fact materialised, although, as already mentioned, it was actually a few miles outside the area we are looking at. The LUT had a very aggressive managing director at that time, a Mr Clifton Robinson, and his planned extension so far into what was then largely open country was a very bold proposal. It was one however which proved to be an immediate success as we shall see later. We should remind ourselves that in 1898, there were barely 1,000 miles of tramway in operation over the country as a whole and most of that was horse or steam traction. 1898 was also the year in which the very first motor bus service in the whole of the UK was inaugurated so the early developments which will unfold in our area should all be seen in this context.

```
THE SLOUGH & WINDSOR 'BUS.

THE new covered-in 'BUS runs between Windsor
    and Slough daily at the undermentioned times:
    FROM WINDSOR.            FROM SLOUGH.
      11.30 a.m.              †10.30 a.m.
       2.45 p.m.                2 0  p.m.
       4 15  ,,                 3.30  ,,
      *6.30  ,,                 5.30  ,,
       8 30  ,,                 7.30  ,,
    *On Sunday 6.5.          †Not on Sunday.

Garden-chair and every other description of brakes
and private carriages for private parties.

            G. M. MARTIN,
      72, WINDSOR ROAD, SLOUGH.
                                        D21/9
```

1) - *Advertisement for a horse-drawn bus service which appeared in 3rd February 1899 edition of the Windsor Chronicle; the use of the word 'bus', particularly in its abbreviated form, was unusual at this early stage.*

Also coincidentally in that same year, another London based enterprise was putting out potential feelers, this time right into the heart of Windsor. The London Steam Omnibus Company was formed at the end of June, 1898 and its prospectus spoke of daily services from London to the Royal Borough, among other destinations. The sight of buses powered by steam, puffing and wheezing their way up Thames Street, Windsor to their terminus at Castle Hill is difficult to imagine these days. It was not so fanciful however because as a matter of fact, although not mentioned in the local papers, the Great Western Railway ('G.W.R.'), of which we shall soon hear a great deal more, tried out Clarkson steam buses on all their Slough based operations in 1905, although not, apparently, with great success.

In 1901, the first of two local tramway proposals emerged, both intended to link Slough to the metropolis. Like the steam car scheme before it, it was to prove abortive, but it was serious enough to warrant the formation of a new company in December that year to be known as The Hounslow, Slough and Datchet Light Railway Company. As its name implies, the object of this new company, which was promoted by the already existing Metropolitan District Electric Traction Company, was to build a line from Hounslow Barracks underground station, out along the Bath Road, through Colnbrook, as far as Slough. Slough was a market town in those days with no particular industrial bias; it only had a population of some 11,000 and the absence of industry meant that there was no particular commuting demand. There were however, a number of communities along the intervening Bath Road and under this proposal, additional passengers were to be gleaned from a branch line which was to come off at Colnbrook and turn south down to the river at Datchet.

The second of the two abortive tramway schemes surfaced in the following year and proved to be a proposal which came very close to fulfilment. In May 1902, the LUT, which by now was well advanced with its Uxbridge project, tabled a light railway order proposal for an extension from Hounslow, the western limit of their existing development on that axis, again through Colnbrook, to Slough. Like the Metropolitan proposal referred to above, the line was to serve such centres of population as there were along the old Bath Road, but there the similarity ended because the LUT scheme was to extend even further west, through Taplow to Maidenhead. When one reflects on how much open country there was in those days between those towns and on the extremely rural nature of the route being contemplated, to talk of running trams out as far as Maidenhead must have been a truly breathtaking proposal. Once again, as in the 1901 Metropolitan plan, there was to be a branch line to Datchet, the terminus being the Manor Hotel, standing as it still does today on the edge of the picturesque green, plus in this plan, another branch to Langley (North Star Hotel).

Datchet, with its riverside setting, must have been quite a magnet in those days for visitors and potential residents; its size alone would surely not have justified two tramway companies specifically planning to bring it into their network. Its attractiveness is confirmed by the fact that around 1907, the G.W.R. was promoting Datchet as a place of residence for commuters even though the London and South Western Railway Company actually served it and the nearest G.W.R. Station was Slough, with no bus service between the two places, either motorised or horse-drawn.

As to Maidenhead, the ultimate destination of this most ambitious tramway project, it must surely have been the weekend tourist traffic potential which attracted the LUT Board to contemplate such a far-flung destination. At around this time, Maidenhead was a very fashionable place and a tremendous magnet for Londoners. Apart from day trippers, however, people were not generally in the habit of commuting to work by road over what, in those days, would have been considered to be appreciable distances. The line was scheduled to cross the river over the bridge which is still there today, and proceed into the town to a terminus outside the Bear Hotel, also still in existence. Users of the bridge still had to pay a toll at that time and this continued to be the case up to 1905. The G.W.R. objected to the proposal, not

MOTOR CARS FOR SLOUGH AND THE DISTRICT.

IMPORTANT PROPOSALS BY THE GREAT WESTERN RAILWAY COMPANY.

Next Tuesday, the 1st of March, the Great Western Railway Company will inaugurate a service of road motor cars between Slough Station and Beaconsfield, via Stoke Road, Stoke Poges, Farnham Royal, and Farnham Common in connection with their excellent service of fast trains to London, Maidenhead, Reading, etc.

The cars are handsome vehicles of the omnibus type, with accommodation for luggage, and are driven by 20 h.p. petrol engines of the most improved design. One of them has been exhibited at the Automobile Show at the Crystal Palace, and a picture of it appeared in last Saturday's "Illustrated London News."

As a commencement three cars will be employed, one running from Beaconsfield to Slough three times daily in each direction, while the others will run between Slough Station and Farnham (Post Office) at more frequent intervals throughout the day. On the Beaconsfield service the first car will leave Beaconsfield at about 8.30 a.m., connecting with the 9.58 a.m. fast train to Paddington. There will be a trip about mid-day from Slough, and a return trip from Beaconsfield about 4.30 p.m., while the last car will leave Slough Station at 8.15 p.m. in connection with the 5.45 p.m. fast train from Paddington.

On the Farnham Royal service the first car will arrive at Slough Station in time for passengers to catch the 9.2 a.m. fast train for Paddington, and the last trip from Farnham Royal will be about 8 p.m.

2) - Extract from the report of the first motor bus service in 27th February 1904 edition of the Slough Observer surprisingly, because the fares would have seriously undercut their rail fares and the LUT was forced to go back to Parliament for a new Bill which was duly tabled in 1904.

Meanwhile, in 1903 there had been stirrings in the motor bus side of the industry which were to have a fundamental bearing on our area. The G.W.R., the prince among railway companies, started its first motor bus service on 17th August 1903. Although this was a long way away, down in Cornwall, the success of that first foray into the operation of feeder bus services encouraged the G.W.R. to repeat the process a little over six months later in the area we are looking at, when they inaugurated their first feeder service to and from Slough on 1st March 1904.

Before we get on to that, however, we must just close the saga of the Slough/Maidenhead tram proposal. In the Slough Observer during the months of January and February 1904, all the talk was of the coming of the electric trams and what a benefit they would be to the local communities. The doubtful elements in the local council chambers wondered how they would ever attract enough customers; as evidence of this, one councillor recounted that he had only passed five tramps and two carts on a journey he had recently made, presumably in a motor car, along the road from Slough to Taplow. To this kind of comment, the other lobby responded with the argument which has been used many times since in this same context, namely that the new service would naturally create its own demand.

The Windsor Express of 2nd January 1904 stated quite categorically that, whereas the London United Tramways were hoping to eventually reach Reading with their line through Slough, they would definitely be building a spur line up to Burnham Beeches. Such a thought is nowadays absolutely mind-boggling - even then they wrestled with the thought of 'electric cars invading the quiet Buckinghamshire lanes'.

However enthusiastically the populace awaited their emancipation, their councillors and local authority officials were not to be taken in lightly; as a matter of fact, they were very

3) - G.W.R. Motor bus AF64, licensed in Cornwall in February 1904, at the northern terminus of the first motorised service in the area, namely the White Hart in Beaconsfield Old Town, still there today.

demanding in their conditions of acceptance for the new service. At the end of January, the LUT appeared to be prepared to go along with Slough Borough Council's requirements and those of other local authorities along the route and although Slough Council had lodged a formal objection to the plan, this was said to be a mere formality and a meeting was scheduled 'within a week' with the LUT representatives to discuss the details. It must, therefore, have come as quite a shock to people at that time, to read in the local paper dated 27th February 1904, that the LUT had abandoned its Slough/Maidenhead route due to the excessive demands of the local councils along the way. Just how much of a shock it is difficult for us to visualise as we now take for granted our individual mobility in the shape of a car.

Apparently Slough Council had insisted on the whole of the relevant roads being properly surfaced from kerb to kerb as opposed to the more normal arrangements under which the tramway company only paid for the space to be surfaced between the rails and a limited area on either side. We must remember that unsurfaced roads were the norm for several more years to come. It had also asked for the power conduits to be laid underground through the whole of the Borough instead of, as was also more normal both at that time, and indeed so far as the suburbs were concerned, right up to the time of London Transport tramway abandonment, in the form of overhead wiring. These demands, plus others for road widening from neighbouring Colnbrook and other local authorities, had been financially too much for the LUT Managing Director to bear and he withdrew that part of his 1904 Bill, leaving only a line to Staines as a possibility; this latter scheme was sanctioned by the Act which was finally approved on 15th August 1904, but it never came to pass.

Meanwhile, somewhat symbolically, since events across the country as a whole have subsequently shown that the electric tram was finally killed off by the greater mobility of the motor bus, the same edition of the Windsor Express which announced the demise of the tram scheme also, somewhat diffidently it must be said, reported on the forthcoming introduction of the first motor bus service in the area. The report stated that "as from next week, on the 1st March, that much respected company, the G.W.R. would be introducing a service 'of motor cars of the omnibus type' (20 horse-power petrol driven vehicles) from Slough Station to Beaconsfield (White Hart Hotel)". It must be remembered that in those days, and indeed up to relatively recent times, the centre of Old Beaconsfield would have been approached from the south along Windsor End, now a quiet backwater sealed off by the M40, rather than from the east, as it is today.

In this preliminary announcement, it was stated that the service would operate via Stoke Road, Slough; Stoke Poges, Farnham Royal and Farnham Common. There were to be three vehicles used on the service with one making three return journeys a day over the whole length of the route and the other two operating between Slough and Farnham Common 'at more frequent intervals'. The vehicles were to carry not only passengers and their accompanied luggage, but also unaccompanied parcels; this latter aspect was made much of in the report and welcomed in the editorial as being of great potential benefit to the local tradesmen. In fact, it was noted that the parcels could be handed in at parcels receiving offices at Farnham Common and Beaconsfield, apart from the Slough terminus.

The single fare for the whole journey was 1/- (equal to 5 new pence), with other intermediate fares as, for example, from the Yew Tree (a pub still there today, about a mile north of Farnham Common) to Slough 9d., 4d. from Stoke Poges church and 2d. from Salt Hill, where the Three Tuns was and still is. Those who know Slough will realise that there is some contradiction in the route to be taken as between Stoke Road, as mentioned in the preliminary announcement, and Salt Hill; apparently both routes were used almost immediately from the start of operations. Reverting to fares, books of 24 tickets were also available, at a discount; this seems pretty imaginative for those early days, considering that London Transport has only come round to it in fairly recent years; as an example, 24 1/- journeys could be purchased in advance for a guinea, that is to say, one pound and one shilling.

4) - The same bus at the southern terminus of the route, namely Slough station. Initially, the livery of the buses was the same as the G.W.R. train carriages, that is to say, chocolate and cream, but within ten years, the green of the rail locomotives was adopted.

One of the reasons why the G.W.R. focused on Slough as a starting point for one of their earliest motor omnibus services might have been the fact that they had been operating a service of horse buses from the station there to Burnham Beeches and to Beaconsfield as far back as the summer of 1889 so they had had 15 years in which to judge the passenger potential. Turning the clock back to early June that year, the Windsor Express had reported on the imminent introduction of the service to the Beeches, noting that if successful, the G.W.R. would consider extending it to Beaconsfield. By September, it was said that the service to the Beeches had proved a great success, the buses terminating at the tea gardens in the centre of the common. In the same report, it was confirmed that some of the weekend buses had continued to Beaconsfield and this was to be a permanent extension from the summer of 1890 onwards. The 1891 Kelly's directory reported that there were three departures a day from Slough station to Burnham Beeches (the operator was not mentioned), but it did not refer to any journeys continuing onto Beaconsfield. The 1895 directory had the same entry, but on the other hand, the local paper of 1st May 1892 referred to the start (possibly re-start) of the G.W.R. bus service to Beaconsfield. The 1903 directory still noted the three departures daily to Burnham Beeches.

However, we must revert to the motor bus services and the 1904 inauguration. In the Slough Observer of 5th March that year, published just five days after the service had started, the paper congratulated the G.W.R. on its new enterprise, describing the buses as 'handsome cars which run most easily' and again referring to the tremendous convenience of the parcel service. The reference to the quality of the vehicles is not surprising in that one of them had been on the Milnes-Daimler stand at the 1904 Commercial Vehicle Show and its bodywork was by Thrupp and Maberley, for many years one of the most distinguished coachwork companies.

The significance of a motor bus service as early as 1904 cannot be exaggerated. These really were the pioneer days of such services - after all the first service in London only started in 1899 - and the number of places served by motor bus over the country as a whole could still be counted on relatively few fingers. The citizens of Slough and district were very fortunate indeed and although trains were now obviously well established in the Home Counties, having the facility of a motor bus service in a rural area was still very exceptional; even in central London, horse buses were to predominate for another five years at least.

The full timetable of the new service was revealed in this 5th March edition of the local paper. According to the report, the departures from the Beaconsfield end - the property developers of the day described both the Beaconsfield and Gerrards Cross areas as 'The Brighton of Bucks' and, therefore, highly desirable places of residence - were at 8.30a.m. 12.00 noon and 3.30 p.m. and from the Slough end at 9.55 a.m., 1.30 p.m. and 6.15 p.m. The report also stated that the journey time was one hour. However, neither the journey time nor the actual departure timings were correct as we can see from the official March 1904 time table on page 8. This shows the journey time as only 45 minutes. Even 60 minutes would be very creditable, considering firstly what elementary vehicles these early buses were (they all had solid tyres) and secondly the state of the roads in those days. On the other hand, traffic jams were probably not a major problem! The timetable also shows additional journeys to the One Pin via Stoke Poges, but none specifically to Farnham Common. The One Pin pub which is still there today, as is the Fox and Pheasant incidentally, was the nearest point to Hedgerley village, as the timetable suggests.

As feeder services to the railhead at Slough, it was obviously logical that the first journey of the day should come from the other end, so to speak, so as to catch certain trains (actually specified in the newspaper report); conversely, the last journey was scheduled to meet certain evening arrivals. The interesting aspect of this, however, is where was the vehicle kept overnight - did it run light up to Beaconsfield first thing or, more likely, was there a dormy shed (an unmanned lock-up garage) there, or some other arrangement, from the start of operations? The White Hart may well have let the G.W.R. park the bus in their yard.

There are several comments that one could make from a perusal of the timetable. One is that it was apparently the practice then, and indeed for 20 or 30 years to come in the case of small bus operators, to not show the timings for all the intermediate points on the route; this must surely have been due to an unwillingness to commit the operator rather than idleness on the part of the compiler. Secondly, the G.W.R. must have had total faith in the punctuality of their railway trains to only allow one minute in some cases between the arrival time of the train and the departure of the connecting bus. The reverse did not apparently apply as the bus was usually given some 6 or 7 minutes leeway to connect with the train; the company actually waived any responsibility for late running of the buses in one of the footnotes to the timetable.

Great Western Railway

MOTOR OMNIBUSES
BETWEEN
SLOUGH STATION, STOKE POGES,
FARNHAM & BEACONSFIELD

SLOUGH AND BEACONSFIELD—WEEK DAYS.

		A.M.	P.M.	P.M.	P.M.			A.M.	P.M.	P.M.	P.M.
PADDINGTON	dep.	9 15	1 0	5 5	6 35	BEACONSFIELD (White Hart Hotel)	dep.	8 45	12 25	4 30	6 30
SLOUGH	arr.	9 51	1 24	5 29	6 59	YEW TREE INN		...	...	...	Via "One Pin" and Stoke
SLOUGH	dep.	9 55	1 30	5 30	7 0	FARNHAM COMMON (Post Office)	about	9 0	12 40	4 45	
SALT HILL		...	...	...	...	FARNHAM ROYAL	,,	9 5	12 45	4 50	
FARNHAM ROYAL	about	10 20	1 55	(Via Stoke see below)	7 25	SALT HILL		...	...	...	
FARNHAM COMMON (Post Office)	,,	10 25	2 0		7 30	SLOUGH STATION		9 30	1 10	5 15	7 10
YEW TREE INN		...	...		...	SLOUGH	dep.	9 38	1 17	5 30	7 14
BEACONSFIELD (White Hart Hotel)	arr.	10 40	2 15	6 15	7 45	PADDINGTON	arr.	10 3	1 45	6 0	7 50

SLOUGH AND "ONE PIN" FOR HEDGERLEY via STOKE—WEEK DAYS.
(Also BEACONSFIELD via STOKE.)

		A.M.	A.M.	P.M.	P.M.						P.M.
PADDINGTON	dep.	7 45	10 10	2 0	5 5	BEACONSFIELD	dep.	...	...	...	6 30
SLOUGH	arr.	8 25	10 38	2 29	5 29	YEW TREE INN	,,	...	...	...	...
SLOUGH STATION	dep.	8 35	10 40	2 30	5 30			A.M.	A.M.	P.M.	
STOKE GREEN		...	...	...	...	"ONE PIN" for HEDGERLEY	dep.	9 5	11 30	3 25	6 50
STOKE CHURCH (Cross Roads)		...	...	...	...	STOKE COMMON (Fox and Pheasant)		...	...	...	...
STOKE POGES VILLAGE (Sefton Arms)		...	...	...	...	STOKE POGES VILLAGE (Sefton Arms)		...	...	...	...
STOKE COMMON (Fox and Pheasant)		...	...	...	...	STOKE CHURCH (Cross Roads)		...	...	...	...
"ONE PIN" for HEDGERLEY	arr.	9 0	11 5	2 55	5 55	STOKE GREEN		...	...	...	...
YEW TREE INN		—	—	—	...	SLOUGH STATION	about	9 30	11 55	3 50	7 15
BEACONSFIELD		—	—	—	6 15	SLOUGH	dep.	9 38	12 4	3 57	7 35
						PADDINGTON	arr.	10 3	12 42	4 25	8 10

The Omnibuses will call at the intermediate places shown. Passengers may also join at any other point on payment of fare from previous stage.

FARES:

BETWEEN	Slough Station.	Salt Hill.	Farnham Royal.	Farnham Common.	Yew Tree Inn.	Beaconsfield.
SLOUGH STATION	—	2d.	3d.	3d.	9d.	1/0
SALT HILL	2d.	—	4d.	6d.	8d.	1/0
FARNHAM ROYAL	3d.	4d.	—	2d.	4d.	6d.
FARNHAM COMMON	3d.	6d.	2d.	—	2d.	6d.
YEW TREE INN	9d.	8d.	4d.	2d.	—	4d.
BEACONSFIELD	1/0	1/0	6d.	6d.	4d.	—

BETWEEN	Slough Station.	Stoke Green.	Stoke Poges Church.	Stoke Poges Village.	Stoke Common.	"One Pin."	Beaconsfield.
SLOUGH STATION	—	3d.	4d.	6d.	6d.	9d.	1/0
STOKE GREEN	3d.	—	2d.	4d.	4d.	8d.	1/0
STOKE POGES CHURCH (Cross Roads)	4d.	2d.	—	2d.	4d.	6d.	9d.
STOKE POGES VILLAGE (Sefton Arms)	6d.	4d.	2d.	—	2d.	4d.	8d.
STOKE COMMON (Fox and Pheasant)	6d.	6d.	4d.	2d.	—	2d.	6d.
"ONE PIN" for HEDGERLEY	9d.	8d.	6d.	4d.	2d.	—	4d.
BEACONSFIELD	1/0	1/0	9d.	8d.	6d.	4d.	—

TICKETS will be issued on the Omnibuses, and must be retained until completion of journey.

BOOKS OF 24 TICKETS at the undermentioned reduced scale of charges can be obtained at the Booking Office at Slough Station:—
- Between Slough Station and Beaconsfield ... 21/-
- ,, Slough Station and Farnham Common (Post Office) ... 14/-
- ,, Slough Station and Stoke Poges Village ... 10/6

FULL FARES TO BE PAID FOR ALL SEATS OCCUPIED.

TIME TABLES.—The Directors give notice that the Company do not undertake that the Motor Omnibuses shall start or arrive at the time specified in the Bills; nor will they be accountable for any loss, inconvenience, or injury, which may arise from delay or detention.

BICYCLES will be carried, when they can be conveyed by the Omnibuses without inconvenience to Passengers, at a charge of 6d. each.

THROUGH RAILWAY TICKETS WILL NOT BE ISSUED ON, NOR BY, THESE MOTOR OMNIBUSES.

PASSENGERS LUGGAGE.—Hand Luggage will be carried free.
Heavy or bulky luggage which can be conveyed by the Motor Omnibuses will be charged for at the rate of 2d. or 4d. per package, according to size or weight, between Slough and Farnham Common (Post Office) or Stoke Common, and 4d. or 6d. per package, according to size or weight, between Slough and Yew Tree Inn and "One Pin" or Beaconsfield.

PARCELS.—Parcels will be conveyed by the Motor Omnibuses between Slough Station, Stoke Poges, Farnham Royal, Farnham Common, and Beaconsfield at the following rates:—
- Up to 7lbs. in weight ... 2d.
- 7lbs. to 28lbs. in weight ... 3d.
- 28 lbs. to 56 lbs. in weight ... 4d.
- 56 lbs. to 112 lbs. in weight ... 6d.

PARCELS AGENTS.—Mr. Thos. Dunkin, Farnham Royal; Messrs. Spong and Purser, Farnham Common; Mr. T. F. Lane, Beaconsfield.

For any further information respecting the arrangements shown in this handbill, application should be made to Mr. W. A. Hart, Divisional Superintendent, Paddington Station.

PADDINGTON, March, 1904.

JAMES C. INGLIS, General Manager.

WYMAN & SONS, Ltd., Printers, Fetter Lane, London, E.C., and Reading.—9851a.

5) - The official March 1904 timetable for the first motor bus route in the area.

We should remember that prior to the introduction of this service, the only way to get from Beaconsfield to London was by stage coach, either direct to London down the Oxford Road (now the A40) or back to High Wycombe and thence by rail over the circuitous route via Bourne End and Cookham to Maidenhead, where the same main line which passed through Slough, could be joined.

The local paper for the following week was still, not unnaturally, fairly full of the new service although, as noted earlier, it had announced its introduction in a fairly unemotional way. It reported that on one of the journeys which had been observed that week, the bus was 'filled to overflowing which ultimately resulted in a second car for Farnham Village'. It also talked of the possibility of the G.W.R. establishing workshops at Slough for its road vehicle fleet, a possibility which actually turned into a reality, as we shall see, in the following year.

That same edition of the paper also contained an editorial which talked about the coming of the 'season of dust' on the roads and what a menace to the general health of the population this represented. It exhorted the Slough Borough Council to have all its available water carts ready and prepared to combat this pollution. This is a fascinating reminder of the conditions under which these early services were being operated. It is also fascinating to recall that it was only on 1st March 1905 that the requirement for having a man with a red flag walking in front of every vehicle in excess of three tons was raised to five tons, thus permitting the development of the double decker bus. The G.W.R. had apparently got round this weight restriction on their early double deckers by removing sufficient equipment from the vehicle when it was being registered and then replacing it - this practice was apparently regarded as quite legitimate!

Three months to the day after the first motor bus service started, the first (and only) tram service we are concerned about, was inaugurated, albeit a few miles outside our area. The LUT completed the line to Uxbridge at the end of May 1904 and after the necessary trial runs, the public service started on 1st June. Thus LUT route 7 was born; the journey time to Shepherds Bush was 81 minutes and the service frequency soon became every 8-10 minutes. Initially, the fare was only 5d. and this was obviously regarded as a bargain even in those days; it does after all compare very favourably with the G.W.R. fares mentioned earlier.

This route constitutes the only service which actually materialised in or near the area we are looking at which was operated by trams and subsequently trolley buses. One can however speculate that if Slough, which developed so rapidly in the '20s and '30s, had been further from London, it would have almost certainly had its own corporation transport department. We know that even as late as 1936, three years after London Transport had taken a virtual monopoly of bus operation in the area, the Borough Council were still regretting the fact they did not own a municipal bus fleet instead of having to put up with the unsatisfactory services provided by the London intruder. Had there been such a transport department, it might well have followed the path of tramway and later trolley bus operation and so Burnham Beeches would have almost certainly been connected by overhead wires, if not by rails.

Burnham Beeches was, in any case, to remain a popular public transport destination for many years, with services specifically serving the Beeches and terminating at Wingrove's Tea Gardens right up to 1952.

CHAPTER 2

Within three weeks of the news that the projected tram service through Slough to Maidenhead had been dropped, the local paper was already taking quite a favourable view of the outcome. The editorial was of the opinion that the potential pluses were more than out-numbered by the potential minuses so that in their estimation, it was no bad thing that the plan had fallen through. It was, however, pointed out that the construction phase would have provided considerable local employment over quite a long period. Meanwhile, the fledgling motor bus service to Beaconsfield was apparently being well patronised, but it was noted that it was still not possible to obtain a through booking from Beaconsfield to Paddington; although this was obviously regarded as something which would come in due course, it never did happen, to my knowledge.

In the local paper of 19th March, 1904, a G.W.R. application to store petrol at Slough station was reported as having been granted, up to a maximum of 500 gallons. This was surely indicative of plans for expansion from the Slough rail-head, because with the then existing level of road activity, it would have taken some two months to consume that quantity. On the other hand, it is almost certain that there would have been no other sources of fuel along the way.

Also in March that year, a traffic census was carried out on the Thames road bridge linking Windsor and Eton; this bridge is still there today, but it is now pedestrianised. (Only five and a half years prior to this census, users of the bridge would have had to pay a toll). Apparently, a total of 7,670 vehicles had crossed the bridge in one week, presumably in both directions, and this represented an increase of 25% over the previous census in 1900. The fascinating aspect however is that of this total, only 121 were motor cars or motorised vehicles (to my knowledge, no buses on service). This is a good reminder of the predominance of the horse-drawn vehicle at this time, a situation which was to continue for some years. On the other hand, in the same year of 1904, an A.A. man started patrolling the Slough section of the London to Bath Road at the weekends so motor cars were obviously beginning to be slightly more plentiful.

In 9th April 1904 local paper, it was announced that one of the G.W.R. 'cars' would be operating from Slough Station through Stoke Poges to the One Pin pub near Hedgerley which as mentioned earlier still stands there today. Based on the timetable illustrated on page 8 the paper was apparently just catching up on these alternative journeys. The same report confirmed that the Beaconsfield cars continued to operate via Farnham Royal. Since the early thirties, there has not been a bus service between Stoke Common and the One Pin; for at least the last 60 years, this pub and the village of Hedgerley beyond it have been approached from the junction off the Beaconsfield road at the other end of One Pin Lane, known as Hedgerley Corner.

It appears that a number of variations on the Slough-Beaconsfield theme were being tried out around this time. How the journeys, which ran through Stoke Poges and on to Beaconsfield got back on to the main road is not clear; they could have either come down One Pin Lane and turned right on to what is now the A355 at Hedgerley Corner, or they could have cut through Parish Lane and emerged on to the same road at the Yew Tree. Judging by the fare structure, I believe it is the latter route which they would have taken. Generally, however, the pattern settled down to operating to Beaconsfield either via Stoke Green or via Salt Hill; Stoke Poges was usually served separately by buses terminating there or going on as far as the One Pin. However, the fact remains the timetable shows one through journey a day in each direction operating via Stoke Poges.

Also in one of the April 1904 editions, the Slough Observer reported that the Luff's penny timetable for May (Luff's were actually the proprietors of the newspaper at the time) would include, for the first time, the timings of the motor omnibuses between Slough and Beaconsfield, in addition to the usual train times.

The May 7th paper noted that "the G.W.R. cars are always crowded both ways". It also contained a letter from a reader which gave an interesting new angle on their area of operation; he noted that apart from the obvious delights of travelling through beautiful scenery, which the G.W.R. had effectively opened up, they were actually 'occupying the ground against threatened attack' from the London and South Western Railway Company which, according to this correspondent, was thinking of building a line from Ascot northwards to connect with the Metropolitan extension to Amersham; this would have passed right through the district currently being wooed by the motor bus and presumably connected Beaconsfield by rail, to London, albeit, probably, with a change of train

6) - G.W.R. bus BH 269 outside the White Hart in Beaconsfield; the registration record of this bus, dated 6th April 1904, can still be seen at Buckinghamshire County Records Office in Aylesbury, Slough being within that county in those days.

Returning to our new bus service, the paper stated two weeks later that, in anticipation of expected demand on the forthcoming Whit-Monday, it was planned to operate 13 journeys each way on the route (but at usual fares); in the event, it was reported the following week that this had still proved inadequate to cope with the demand. Obviously, travelling in a motorised vehicle was still a great novelty for the vast majority of people and to actually travel reasonably comfortably from Slough to Beaconsfield (a delightful town to the present day) was an irresistible temptation. Presumably, the local taverns benefitted from this new influx of visitors.

However, one or two words of mild criticism were beginning to creep into the letters to the paper on the subject - one lamented the fact the journeys back to Slough were often running late, only allowing the passengers one or two minutes to get over the bridge to their 'connecting' trains to London. Obviously, the leeway referred to in the last chapter was proving necessary. Another letter expressed regret that with so many people now having access to Burnham Beeches, flowers and plants were being carted away by visitors, thus destroying the natural untouched beauty of the place. This sentiment, in a way, finds a parallel in more recent times in the fears of many people that the M6 motorway would open up the Lake District to too many motorists - nobody appreciates other folk being able to enjoy what one enjoys oneself!

One of these correspondents noted gratefully that there was 'no service on the Sabbath' on the bus route, but by an apparent coincidence, the G.W.R. announced the following week that as from 5th June, 1904, Sunday services would be initiated - also with four journeys each way.

The first week of July, 1904, it was reported that the One Pin service was being withdrawn but the service 'in this direction' would run as far as the Sefton Arms, Stoke Poges (interestingly, the modern replacement pub on the site, now called The Six Bells, was briefly re-christened Seftons in 1984). Perhaps the residents of Hedgerley preferred to remain faithful to their long established horse-bus service (of which, more anon), rather than walk as far as the One Pin. As mentioned earlier, some buses going through to Beaconsfield were now serving Stoke Green in addition to those only going as far as Stoke Poges village. Although not mentioned in the local paper, there were apparently some journeys which came up to Stoke Green and then along Park Road to join what is now the A355 at Farnham Royal, before turning north.

In that same paper was the first hint of a new motor bus service to Windsor. Its introduction, which was being delayed, was apparently an exercise on the part of the G.W.R. to see whether Chalvey, which is between Slough and Eton and which would be served by the new service, would generate enough custom to justify building a railway halt there on the G.W.R.'s existing Slough-Windsor line. (Such a halt was eventually built adjacent to the road bridge, but not until 25 years later; even then, it only remained open just over a year, presumably and ironically rendered superfluous by the later proliferation of bus operators over the route).

Sure enough, it was duly announced that as from Monday, 18th July, 1904, a new G.W.R. bus service would be introduced between Slough station and Windsor (G.W.R. station), via Eton. There were to be 13 journeys a day each way, the first leaving Slough at 9.00am and the last returning from the Royal Borough at 9.30pm - evidently no thought of carrying people to their work in either direction first thing in the morning. The fare was 2d single to Eton and 3d to Windsor; even better, 24 3d. tickets could be bought in advance for 5s.6d, or 27½ current pence. This time, the paper got it right as the timetable illustrated on page 14 confirms these reports and also the fact that, as on the Beaconsfield service, through railway tickets were not available.

Apparently, the buses used to leave Slough station and initially go eastwards along the old Wellington Street (not the racetrack which bears that name today), before turning down Wexham Road and coming back along the High Street as far as Crown Corner; they then set off for Eton. At that stage, however, the return journeys to Slough used to go straight back down Mackenzie Street, which is now buried under the Queensmere shopping centre, to terminate at the station.

The following week, the paper reported on the introduction of the service and stated that it was being maintained by 'a double-decker' - the quotes are theirs; this vehicle had apparently only lasted a day before breaking down on the Tuesday morning and remaining out of service until the Wednesday evening. However, that did not seem to prevent the service being generally well patronised. As previously mentioned, double deckers were, strictly speaking, illegal until 1st March, 1905, when the new Heavy Motor Car Order came into effect, raising the maximum weight from three to five tons. However, there were ways to get round these things, by all accounts!

7) - One of the earliest G.W.R. double decker buses used on the service from Slough to Windsor, having been licensed at Aylesbury less than a month before the service began.

This service was the first motorised bus route to reach Windsor and apart from the very transient Hayward and Hill service referred to in Chapter 5, it was in fact the only one to do so for another eight years. It should also be remembered that it would have come down Eton High Street, over the river bridge into Thames Street and then climbed the hill up to the station.

GREAT WESTERN RAILWAY.

MOTOR OMNIBUSES

BETWEEN

SLOUGH and WINDSOR STATIONS

(VIA ETON).

Commencing on Monday July 18th, Motor Omnibuses will run between the above points as under:

SLOUGH TO WINDSOR.—Week Days.

	a.m.	a.m.	a.m.	noon	p.m.	p.m.	p.m.	p.m.	p.m.	p.m.	p.m.	p.m.	p.m.
Slough Station - dep.	9. 0	10. 0	11. 0	12. 0	1. 0	2. 0	3. 0	4. 0	5. 0	6. 0	7. 0	8. 0	9. 0
Windsor (G.W.) Station - arr. abt.	9.15	10.15	11.15	12.15	1.15	2.15	3.15	4.15	5.15	6.15	7.15	8.15	9.15

WINDSOR TO SLOUGH.—Week Days.

	a.m.	a.m.	a.m.	noon	p.m.	p.m.	p.m.	p.m.	p.m.	p.m.	p.m.	p.m.	p.m.
Windsor (G.W.) Station - dep.	9.30	10.30	11.30	12.30	1.30	2.30	3.30	4.30	5.30	6.30	7.30	8.30	9.30
Slough Station arr. abt.	9.45	10.45	11.45	12.45	1.45	2.45	3.45	4.45	5.45	6.45	7.45	8.45	9.45

The Motor Omnibuses will run via High Street, Slough, and call at Eton and other points as required in each direction.

FARES:

Between Slough and Windsor - - - - - 3d.
Between Slough and Eton or Windsor and Eton - - 2d.

Single Tickets only will be issued on the Motor Omnibuses and must be retained until completion of the journey.

Books of 24 Tickets, available by the Company's Omnibuses between Slough and Windsor, can be obtained at the Booking Offices at Slough and Windsor at a charge of 5s. 6d.

FULL FARES TO BE PAID FOR ALL SEATS OCCUPIED.

TIME TABLES.—The Directors give notice that the Company do not undertake that the Motor Omnibuses shall start or arrive at the time specified in the Bills; nor will they be accountable for any loss, inconvenience, or injury, which may arise from delay or detention.

THROUGH RAILWAY TICKETS WILL NOT BE ISSUED ON, NOR BY, THESE MOTOR CARS.

For any further information respecting the arrangements shewn in this handbill, application should be made to Mr. W. A. Hart, Divisional Superintendent, Paddington Station.

PADDINGTON, July, 1904.

JAMES C. INGLIS, General Manager.

Wyman & Sons, Ltd., Printers, Fetter Lane, London, E.C., and Reading.—10543a.

8) - The July 1904 timetable for the G.W.R. motor bus service between Slough and Windsor.

This was the route followed by all the subsequent bus services coming into Windsor from the north up to 1970, when the bridge was closed to traffic; since then, bus services have deserted Eton to all intents and purposes in order to use the new "relief road".

Within two weeks of the introduction of the Windsor service, there was talk of another service from Slough along the Bath Road to Colnbrook; this was anticipated to be introduced 'at an early date' although in fact it did not appear until the following year. So confident was the paper that it subsequently reported that the service would be starting on 1st September, 1904, with the possibility of going beyond Colnbrook to Hounslow, through a district 'not touched by either motor or train service'! (So we know nothing had actually materialised along what had seemed, from the Hounslow end, a very attractive route to earlier would-be operators).

Another pipe-dream which in fact **never** came to pass appeared in the G.W.R. magazine for August 1904; this stated that there would 'shortly' be a new service from Windsor through Slough to Maidenhead. Premier eventually ran such a service but never the G.W.R.; in fact, Maidenhead was not to be served by railway company buses, or indeed, any other motor buses, until 1911.

> REDUCTION OF BUS FARES.
> SLOUGH TO WINDSOR.
>
> H. BARRETT,
>
> Proprietor of the Windsor and Slough Buses,
>
> BEGS to inform the general Public that on and after Monday, Sep. 5th, 1904, the Fares for said Buses will be as follows:—
>
> Dolphin Hotel to Windsor Hill .... 3d.
> Crown Hotel to Windsor Hill .... 2d.
> Dolphin Hotel to Arbour Hill .... 1d.
> Arbour Hill to Eton College .... 1d.
> Eton College to Windsor Hill .... 1d.
>
> H. B. wishes to thank his numerous patrons for their past favours, and trusts that by strict attention to their comforts, he will be favoured with continuance of same. 2

9) - Advertisement in 17th September 1904 edition of the Slough Observer regarding the fare reduction in the horse bus service.

When the August Bank Holiday arrived, the general public really showed their appreciation of the two new services which were now operating from Slough. No fewer than 1,928 passengers were carried on the two routes and the total fare revenue amounted to £87 - approximately 11 old pence a journey, which means most people were going all the way to Beaconsfield. But this paled into insignificance compared with the Uxbridge trams where apparently no fewer than 10,000 people were carried on that one day; 'cars were arriving every three minutes and the last left Uxbridge at nearly midnight'.

As a matter of fact, the influx of passengers from London was reaching almost crisis proportions with local farmers threatening to 'pepper these unwelcome visitors with gunshot' if they continued to trespass - but that is another story!

Reverting to the new Windsor bus service, an additional early morning journey leaving at 8.00am was introduced in early August, making no fewer than 14 return trips a day; the double decker left Slough on the hour and Windsor on the half hour. One is slightly puzzled by the fact that at one moment, there is no motorised public transport between the three towns and the next, there are journeys once an hour, which if all reports are to be believed, were well patronised. Certainly part of the answer is that up until then, horse drawn buses had fulfilled the need, at any rate between Slough and Windsor, prior to the G.W.R. initiative; for the rest it was, perhaps, another case of the supply creating the demand. In reporting new or more frequent motor bus services, the papers never seemed to comment on any resulting reduction in the horse-bus services.

By the middle of August, 1904, the Windsor service had carried over 12,000 passengers in three weeks of operation and was now transporting some 900 per day, all this apparently without any reported reduction in the number of people travelling by train over the same route. To some extent, the G.W.R. were tapping an entirely new market, given that Eton was not then served by rail, nor ever has been, thanks to the protestations of Eton College.

Meanwhile, the paper and its readers were getting increasingly upset about the speed of private motor cars - it was noted in many columns of a report on a council debate on the subject that there were now no less than 200,000 cars in the country as a whole (this was in fact an enormous exaggeration as there were only some 12,000!) and that the Bath Road was one of the more popular routes. A correspondent stated that the dust raised by a passing car

10) - AF 64 at the most treacherous section of the Slough to Beaconsfield route, namely Dorney Bottom, north of the Yew Tree.

was such that those living along that road could never open their windows during daylight hours. Not for the last time, the Council called for a 10 m.p.h. limit on all cars passing through Slough. For the record, the total numbers of cars which had been registered in Berkshire and Buckinghamshire up to Midsummer Day 1904, were 243 and 146 respectively!

In 27th August paper, it was announced that **all** the journeys on the Beaconsfield route would now go right through to that town, none terminating at Farnham Common as was previously the case. It was also noted that the G.W.R. simply could not get new buses quickly enough - 'the bodies are being built at Swindon' - to cope with the demand for new services; hence, the continuing delay in the introduction of the Colnbrook route. In spite of this, there was talk of a new service starting within two months between West Wycombe and Stokenchurch; such a service which is anyway outside our area, never actually came to pass, although an extended version of it was still being rumoured a year later.

Early in September 1904, a Sunday service was introduced on the Slough to Windsor route, and by the middle of the month, there was talk of a possible service from Windsor on to Ascot. The local paper questioned the viability of such a service, except on race days, and was inclined to suggest that the projected Colnbrook route, the introductory date of which had still not been fixed, would be a better bet and "keep the trams at bay"; so obviously tram routes out from London were still a possibility and perhaps in the light of the Uxbridge experience, now regarded as a bit of a threat!

Reverting to the new Sunday service, it would probably have been very popular with some of the local publicans. Certain licences in those days restricted the sale of intoxicating liquor on Sundays to so called 'travellers', that is to say people who had come from at least four miles away. One can safely assume that the new bus service would have created a welcome addition to the numbers of such thirsty people!

Within six weeks of the start of the G.W.R. motor bus service to Windsor, the proprietor of the Windsor and Slough buses - a Mr H Barrett - announced in a series of weekly advertisements, that he was reducing his fares. There was no mention in these advertisements of the mode of traction of these buses and it is only from the editorial comment that one can confirm one's suspicions that these were the horse-drawn omnibuses which were beginning to feel the pinch from the newly arrived motor buses. Mr Barrett introduced three one penny stages for the whole journey between the Dolphin Hotel, Slough (at the eastern end of the town in the Uxbridge Road) and Windsor Castle; the journey from the Crown Hotel, which was effectively the centre of Slough, to the Royal Borough was only going to be two pence. This compared favourably with the three pence the G.W.R. was charging; clearly however, some people were prepared to pay a premium for the greater speed.

Meanwhile, the new railway line from London was getting nearer to Beaconsfield, thus threatening the original raison d'être for the first motor bus service in the district!

CHAPTER 3

During the last quarter of 1904, nothing of any great significance was reported in the local papers regarding the two G.W.R. bus services to Beaconsfield and Windsor respectively, nor were any new services announced. There were minor proposals from correspondents about changing the timing of certain Beaconsfield journeys so as to provide better train connections and of an additional evening departure from the Slough end. In December, there was some comment - as so frequently the case, supportive of the G.W.R. - on the fact that Beaconsfield Council were starting to fret over the state of their roads, the condition of which they apparently felt was due to the regular passage of the G.W.R. buses. The paper reminded the Council that similar rumblings in Cornwall had, not long previously, led to the County requiring the local authority to face up to its responsibilities! How totally different the attitude of the local papers and of the general populace would be on this topic ten years later when, as we shall see, motor buses were beginning to proliferate.

One very interesting report however at the end of the previous month clearly demonstrated the fertility of the G.W.R's imagination. Notwithstanding their monopoly of motor bus operation in the area, they were apparently, even at that relatively late stage in the development of new railways, considering a branch line coming off the main line at Burnham, up through the Farnhams ('close to Burnham Beeches') and Stoke Poges, over to Fulmer and on through Denham to meet the Uxbridge line at Hillingdon. Since the scheme included the acquisition of 17 acres of Stoke Common, the paper surmised that a station would probably be built there. As we know, the line never actually came to pass, but how differently the character of these communities would have developed, had it done so.

Meanwhile, back on the roads, the Slough Council meetings took a great deal of their time that autumn once again wondering whether to impose a 10 mile an hour limit on all motorised vehicles passing through the Borough. Feelings obviously ran very high, but how quaint it all seems some 90 years on.

Nothing was reported in the local papers during the winter of 1904-5 other than a few complimentary comments about the G.W.R. buses keeping good time and the fact that the 2d. fare stage from Windsor station on the route to Slough had been extended as far as Eton laundry, that is to say the junction with the Datchet road (Pococks Lane). The paper expressed the hope that the fare structure over the whole route would be broken down into three 1d stages rather than the complicated system then in force, which was obviously producing some anomalies.

In March 1905 it was noted that two more "motor cars" - the word "bus" was still far from being universally applied - were now based at Slough station. They were of "particularly ornate design and most luxuriously furnished". One was to be used on the forthcoming Windsor - Ascot route (regarded as a fairly up market service from the start, I suspect) and the other would be available for private hire. This latter vehicle was probably the one known as 'The Gem', the pride and joy of the Slough based fleet. To put that fleet into context, it appears that at the end of 1904, the G.W.R. had a total of 36 motor buses in operation over the whole of their area. This would have been a significant number by any standards in those very early days, all the more so for an operator which was largely serving rural communities.

Sure enough, the next significant development to be reported was the commencement on 5th April of the much heralded service from Windsor to Ascot. Each weekday, including Saturdays, a bus was to set out six times a day through Winkfield and Lovel Hill, returning from Ascot at the same frequency. From the outset, there were two journeys each way on Sundays; the journey time for this route was three quarters of an hour. One of the ornate buses referred to previously, which was in fact a Milnes-Daimler with special double deck bodywork, operated the service and it appears that from an early stage, it was based at a dormy shed at Lovel Hill. Once again, the time scheduled for the journey was very creditable. By the late 1920's, the Thames Valley Traction Company's service over the same route had only shaved 5 minutes off the 45 minutes the early G.W.R. buses were taking.

11) - G.W.R. double decker on the Windsor to Ascot service, initiated in April, 1905.

Being more precise about the actual route, it started at the G.W.R. station in Windsor and went out of the town via the King Edward VII hospital, opposite the site where London Transport built its depot almost 30 years later, past the Prince Albert at Clewer Green and out along the Winkfield Road. Having served Winkfield and Lovel Hill, as previously noted, it went over Ascot Heath into the town itself, passing the Royal Ascot Hotel which stood at the junction which is now a large roundabout in front of Heatherwood Hospital, and terminated as other subsequent bus services did, at the Horse & Groom. Where would bus timetables be without pub names to fasten on to? The route was an instant success and in fact lasted right up to 1931, in spite of the expansion in the area in the inter-war years by the Thames Valley Traction Company. On the Easter Monday soon after it started, it carried no fewer than 700 passengers, compared with 1,000 on the two existing services which started from Slough.

The Ascot service had taken some seven months from its first rumblings to actually materialise. Ten months after **its** first mention, the Colnbrook service finally came to pass. On 8th May, 1905, six journeys a day were initiated from Slough, out through Langley and actually on past Colnbrook, as far as Longford; the fare for the whole journey was 8d.

The terminus at Longford was the Peggy Bedford pub, apparently named after a popular hostess from times gone by; in the nineteenth century, it had been the tavern where Queen Victoria's carriages used to stop to change horses en route from London to Windsor. A pub of that name is still there today, but now on the perimeter of Heathrow Airport; who could ever have imagined such a thing as an airport the day the first G.W.R. bus trundled into Longford. The final claim to fame for the old Peggy Bedford was the fact it marked the western boundary of the Metropolitan Police Traffic area with all the restrictions and controls imposed at that time on motor bus operation which that implied; the G.W.R. were wise to terminate at that point. And so within 15 months of establishing a base at Slough, there were now four services in operation. Unfortunately, however, this was not to last for very long.

12) Single decker on the short-lived G.W.R. Slough to Longford service, commenced in May 1905 and terminated in August that year.

In 3rd June, 1905 edition of the Slough Observer, there was a fascinating report on the economics of motor bus operation in London. Apparently, the operators of the "latest type" of motor omnibus were enjoying a very profitable time; takings were some £10 a day compared with only £2 for a horse drawn bus. The latter had to maintain 11 horses, plus supporting staff, for each vehicle, whereas the daily consumption of 18 gallons of petrol at 6d (2½ current pence) per gallon only cost nine shillings or 45p. A conductor was quoted as saying that he had the 'best job in London' - 9 hours a day, six days a week, for £2 a week, plus a bonus of one shilling for avoiding any accidents. However, it was pointed out in the report that as more buses were 'petrolised' (their word), the average level of takings would decline.

After the 1905 Whitsun holiday, it was reported that no fewer than 1,334 people had travelled on the Slough based bus services that weekend; they had paid a total of £26.16.7 in fares, an average of 5 old pence a journey. In the same month, the fare on the Longford service from Slough station to the William IV at Langley was cut from 4d to 3d. There were bumper loadings on the special journeys from Slough to the Eton playing fields on the last Saturday in June - no fewer than 830 passengers - and the extra cars which ran during Ascot week took over £90. All these fairly inconsequential reports and others like them are evidence of the continuing interest which these very early motor bus services were creating in the community. Once again it can be noted that there never was a report on the horse bus services which were still in existence, at least in those areas where there were no motor buses.

The 8th July, 1905 edition of the Slough Observer noted that the G.W.R. had told Beaconsfield Council very firmly that the benefits of the bus service far outweighed the disadvantage of the wear and tear on their roads. The same Council were endeavouring that month to introduce a 12 m.p.h. speed limit on all motorised vehicles passing through their delightful little town.

In the same paper, there was a report of a serious accident to a bus as it was almost completing its return journey to Slough station, going down Mackenzie Street. The full report read as follows:

"Motor Car Charges a Tree - The G.W.R. motor omnibus from Beaconsfield was proceeding from the High Street to Slough Station on Wednesday evening, when the steering gear went wrong and the car dashed into the first tree on the left-hand side of Mackenzie Street. The petrol tank bursted, (sic) and the spirit took fire. The car was soon in flames and the Fire Brigade hastened to extinguish them. The driver was badly burnt, but the passengers, about a dozen in number, escaped with little more than shock. The omnibus, which was completely wrecked, was afterwards towed to the station."

A week later, four more vehicles were introduced on the Beaconsfield service, three to cover the Farnham Common workings and one as far as Beaconsfield; the latter resulted in the last departure from that end now being at 8.00 pm, passing back through Stoke Green at 8.35 pm. This was of course high summer with the benefit of long evenings.

On 24th July 1905 the Longford service was cut back to Colnbrook. Worse was to come however, because within a month - to be precise, on 19th August - the service stopped altogether. It had only lasted just over three months and was never revived by the G.W.R. Obviously the decision must have been due to inadequate loadings, but there was certainly no competing service along that road, then or for some years to come. Perhaps the G.W.R's own railway line had mopped up most of the traffic although the old Bath Road, which in places ran south of today's A.4, was actually a couple of miles south of the railway line so that was not necessarily the reason.

One fascinating and imaginative feature of these early G.W.R. services was that the drivers could earn themselves a bonus of 1d for every gallon of petrol they saved against the standard consumption of 4 miles to the gallon. Given that, as noted earlier, petrol was only 6d a gallon, quite a substantial proportion of the saving was passed on to the driver. One wonders firstly what the unions would make of such an idea these days, and secondly, whether the drivers resorted to freewheeling to earn their extra pennies.

Also in August 1905, the paper noted that a new G.W.R. map which had been posted up at various stations showed a new motor bus route from Stokenchurch, through West

Wycombe and High Wycombe to Loudwater. As noted in the previous chapter, the possibility of a G.W.R. bus service between Stokenchurch and West Wycombe had been mooted in August 1904, exactly a year earlier, but although the paper was totally confident that this extended service would begin at the start of 1906, once again it has to be said that the G.W.R. never operated such a service, although others did, for at least most of the way, as we shall see.

13) Accident to a G.W.R. bus in Mackenzie Street, Slough in July, 1905; note the ladder to enable luggage to be carried on the roof.

From 18th September onwards, Farnham Common was only to be served by through cars on the Beaconsfield route, signifying a reduction in the service between Slough and the intermediate point.

On the last day of September, 1905, it was reported that the G.W.R, the Metropolitan Railway Company and London United Tramways, who it will be recalled ran the trams out to Uxbridge, were proposing to apply for an extension of their system from Uxbridge to Burnham Beeches, via Iver Heath. Since the potential applicants operated different modes of transport, it is not clear what form the extension would have taken! Needless to say, it never came to pass and most people would presumably have regarded that as a blessing; the thought of trams grinding through the Beeches however, is not unattractive to some of us!

The October 1905 G.W.R. magazine reported that the Company now had 58 passenger road cars (an increase of more than 50% in nine months), plus eight goods motors in operation. In view of the growth of the motor vehicle enterprise, it had been decided to move the headquarters of the division from Paddington to Slough where new offices were being provided and a large running shed and repair shop erected. This surely would have been important news for Slough because it would have signalled the potential for significant new employment opportunities in the town, but surprisingly, I could find no comment to this effect in the local papers. This apart, extensive engineering facilities were duly erected and the building itself actually remained in existence (although in other hands) until November 1981 when it and the adjacent houses in Railway Terrace were demolished to make room, coincidentally, for a new bus garage! The G.W.R. Slough works not only carried out maintenance and repairs on their motorised fleet of buses and goods vehicles, but they were also capable of building new radiators, for example, when the outbreak of hostilities in 1914 prevented replacement radiators being imported from Germany for the Daimler buses. Apparently the vehicles being worked on were usually brought to Slough by rail.

The G.W.R. magazine also stated that during the summer months of 1905, an improved type of motor charabanc or "observation" car would appear on the more important tourist routes of their motor bus system. This apparently included the route through Farnham Common to Beaconsfield but not the route to Windsor. Since this was already served by trains, perhaps it was felt that these new vehicles were better employed elsewhere. The new coaches could accommodate 30 passengers and were closed at the back by glass panels which "obviated any inconvenience from dust". They had a centre gangway and a front entrance and were obviously regarded as the crème de la crème at the time.

In 4th November edition of the paper, there was a report of a G.W.R. double-deck motor which, having arrived in Slough from Windsor at 8.45 in the morning, was the victim of a mishap. Having discharged its passengers 'outside Mr Dent's shop' (Mr Dent appears to have been a tailor and outfitter at 59/61 High Street), it prepared to move off. At this point, it was found that the nearside wheels had sunk into a newly filled post office trench and the 'motor' would not move. A jack was procured from the station but it apparently took several men some hours to get the vehicle moving again. The paper stated incorrectly that when empty, the bus weighed 7 tons 8 cwt; in fact this was more than twice its real weight.

14) G.W.R. bus outside the Yew Tree, a fare stage north of Farnham Common on the Beaconsfield service; the pub is still there under that name, but alas, no yew tree.

The following week it was announced that the Beaconsfield service had undergone "considerable alteration". Once more there were only going to be four trips each way on working days, Saturday being a working day like any other, and two on Sundays. Whether it was the recently introduced evening journey which was being cut out was not made clear. In any case, by mid-December there was a partial reversal of the cutback in the shape of an additional journey from Farnham Common to Slough station every working day morning at 8.25, via Farnham Royal and Salt Hill. The positioning journey, which got the bus to Farnham Common to pick up what we would now call the commuters, left Slough half an hour earlier which is what the timetable had shown as the scheduled time for the journey. This additional facility however could not have been a great success because by the end of January 1906, both journeys had been discontinued.

A recurring theme in December 1905 which, as mentioned earlier, had in fact arisen the previous winter, was to beg the G.W.R. to introduce 1d fares on the Windsor service rather than the 2d minimum which was still in force. The paper was of the opinion that a 1d fare from Slough station to say The Prince of Wales, Chalvey at one end of the route or from Windsor station to Eton College at the other, would encourage a lot of extra custom. Nothing actually changed however until competition arrived in 1912.

So ended 1905, a year of modest expansion, but still only one operator in the area. But once again these were still the very, very early days of motor bus operation, and in that context, Windsor and Slough could count themselves as exceptionally blessed. Perhaps the citizens did realise how fortunate they were - after all, they flocked to use the service - but that sentiment never came through in the newspaper reports. It has to be said however that the G.W.R. as a railway company was very much respected and received regular complimentary mention in most editions.

Chapter 4

It is perhaps surprising that there was no comment in the local press around this time regarding the fact that communities in the district which were not fortunate enough to be served by a motor bus route, and clearly they were in the majority, were not apparently clamouring to acquire one. After all, the motor car was still a remote luxury and although there were some 23,000 over the whole country in 1906, it was likely to remain a luxury for the foreseeable future. Although, as we have seen, there was still talk from time to time of new railway lines, the railway mania of the previous century had largely died down and in any case, it would have been clear to everybody that the railways could never serve every little village and community up and down the land.

The January 1906 edition of the G.W.R's own house magazine was patting itself on the back with reference to the Beaconsfield bus service. The point they were making, and it is a classic example of the benefits of feeder bus services for intending rail passengers, was that that route had actually created a demand at its intermediate point, namely Farnham Common, by enabling what we would today call commuters to travel from there to Paddington in 55 minutes. Not only was the point clearly valid, but the time taken was also very creditable and could not be significantly improved on today, assuming today's operators were sensible enough to revert to the practice of connecting their timings with train departures, to say nothing of actually serving railway stations as opposed to supermarkets.

15) A line-up at Slough station of some of the very early G.W.R. buses; the vehicle on the right is one of the Clarkson steamers which were tried out on the Slough-based services in 1905.

Also that January, the Slough Observer noted that there were three departures from the crossroads near Stoke Poges church en route from the Farnhams to Slough at 9.10 a.m., 2.55 p.m. and 6.20 p.m.. Not many one might say at first sight, but it is three more than there are today! It also shows that although the paper had never announced the route variation as such, at least some of the journeys were using Park Road and Stoke Road, Slough to get to the station rather than going via Salt Hill.

During February and March, attention turned, not surprisingly, to the imminent opening of the new railway line from Marylebone, through Gerrards Cross and Beaconsfield to High Wycombe and beyond. I believe that apart from the Channel Tunnel link, this is regarded as the last main line to be opened in England. When eventually it came into operation on 2nd April 1906, it was stated quite clearly in the local papers that the "G.W.R. motor cars" would continue to operate after the opening of the line. So far as the section between Farnham Common and Beaconsfield was concerned, however, this turned out to be largely untrue. Services on this section on a year round basis only continued, as we shall see, until the end of September in the following year and apart from a brief revival during the summer of 1908 on Wednesdays and Saturdays only, there was to be a gap of some 17 years before the G.W.R. operated again over that route.

16) G.W.R. Milnes - Daimler, licensed in March 1905 with registration number BH 02, at the Ascot terminus of the service from Windsor.

Also in March 1906, there was a rumour circulating to the effect that there would soon be a service of motor omnibuses from the terminus of the electric tramways at Hounslow right through to Maidenhead. This was the same route as had been envisaged three years earlier, but this time it was buses rather than trams. The Slough Observer commented that the citizens of Cippenham - then to the west of Slough, but now engulfed by it - could soon be enjoying cheaper fares to either Slough or Maidenhead. Although it was not said, surely the company intending to operate such a service could only have been the London General Omnibus Company; assuming that to be the case, it actually took another six years for that vast enterprise to appear on the local scene.

Perhaps however the desire of smaller communities to have their own bus service was actually beginning to develop. Also in March 1906, it was reported that Burnham Parish Council had instructed its clerk to write to the G.W.R. asking for a new bus service to be started from there to Taplow station and on to Dorney. So far as I know, there was never a

G.W.R. bus service to Dorney and it was not, as we shall see, until 1914 that the company started what was a very short lived service between Burnham and Taplow, continuing on to Maidenhead as a matter of fact; ten years after that, Burnham and Taplow were linked by a G.W.R. service which emanated from Slough.

In May 1906, two additional journeys were added to the Slough - Windsor service, leaving Slough at 8.30 in the morning and 4.30 in the afternoon, as well as the fourteen previous departures on the hour. Over the Whitsun bank holiday that year, extra "road motor cars" were put on all three local services and there were no fewer than 10 departures on the Monday from Farnham Common into Slough, of which it was noted, six would be going via Stoke Poges. The following week, it was reported that all the buses had been heavily laden. One wonders what these extra buses were doing in between bank holiday weekends, given that the G.W.R. was not a major urban operator with heavy weekday commitments like the London General.

The Windsor service was further augmented in early July; in addition to the hourly pattern from the Slough end from 8 in the morning until 9 at night, returning from Windsor on the half-hour, there was an additional one from there at 8.20 am as well as the 8.30 am departure. Where the vehicle came from is not clear. At the same time, the Windsor/Ascot service was increased to seven trips each way on weekdays, and eight on Saturdays.

The Slough Observer printed a letter in July from a Mr W.H. Ransford of The Lodge, Farnham Royal, which to us makes quite amusing reading, although obviously not to the writer. The text was as follows:

17) - *Advertisement in 11th August 1906 edition of the Slough Observer regarding the horse bus service which effectively linked the northern terminus of the G.W.R. motor bus service in Beaconsfield Old Town with the town's new station.*

"To the Station Master, Great Western Railway, Slough. Dear Sir, - For the information of the department it particularly concerns. I beg to call your attention to a serious accident (which might easily have been fatal to both my coachman and groom) that was caused by the company's motor omnibus last evening near the railway bridge on the Farnham road. The noise made by the motor when passing my carriage at a rapid pace caused my horse to shie on to the footpath, and both men were thrown from the box. Fortunately the reins got caught round the wheels, and so stopped the horses within about a hundred yards of the accident. By great good luck the wheels went over the groom's hat

instead of his head, but it was a near thing, as his head was in his hat. The actual result was a bad shaking for the men, a severe injury to the off hind leg of one of the horses, which will prevent his being used for some time (of course to my great inconvenience), a ruined hat, and livery coat. I do not suggest any undue want of care on the part of the motor driver, but if these cumbrous, noisy vehicles are allowed to be driven at some 12 to 15 miles an hour on the public roads, regardless of whether these are wide or narrow, they are a source of serious danger to all other users of the road."

Rumours of new services - both bus and tram - continued to crop up in the local papers. In August 1906, it was reported that the London & South Western Railway Company proposed to establish a motor bus service from Woking, which was on their main line, to Windsor. I do not think such a service ever came to pass, although some 24 years later, Woking & District initiated an operation over that route and this became the East Surrey service 38 in 1931. And finally, in the tramway context, some unbelievably ambitious schemes were apparently being thought up. The London County Council were considering through electric tram services from Romford to Maidenhead, with off-shoots to Uxbridge and Staines, but none rather surprisingly to Burnham Beeches. I assume that somebody somewhere had worked out how long it would actually take to travel between Romford and Maidenhead by tram - I doubt whether it would have been an attractive proposition for a day out, but meanwhile it made the Hounslow to Maidenhead scheme of 1904 seem positively modest!

Coming down to earth with what actually was happening in our immediate locality, the local paper carried a weekly advertisement from August 1906 onwards, for at least a year, stating that a Mr H Roberts had taken over the "station bus" from Mr Lane of the Royal White Hart, Beaconsfield, which would continue to ply between that hotel and the railway station. It is rather puzzling to think that the G.W.R. had not extended its motor bus service from its original terminus at the White Hart about another three quarters of a mile down the hill to the railway station when the latter came into use earlier that year, particularly since they were one of the companies operating trains on the route. Had they done so, the people of Farnham Common for example, would have had the choice of two possible routes into London. Instead, they apparently allowed the horse-bus shuttle to continue to link the old town of Beaconsfield with its station. Maybe the owner of the White Hart, the previous operator of the horse-bus service, had persuaded them to allow passengers to have the opportunity of taking some refreshment at his inn, before continuing their journey.

Two interesting asides on motor bus operation around this time were noted in the paper. The first was that dust caused by motor buses was settling on the roadside strawberries and giving the people who ate them, diarrhoea! The second was more uplifting, namely that the Financial Times had reported that three of the railway company boards (the G.W.R. was not one of them) had stated that their motor bus operations were unremunerative. The Chairman of the Great Central Railway in particular (the other Beaconsfield line operator) had told his shareholders that feeder bus services were barely economical unless the passenger was also undertaking a long railway journey. In a separate report, it was said that the G.W.R. motor bus fleet had carried no less than 612,873 people during the first half of 1906, so clearly it was a very popular facility, if not a profitable one.

Meanwhile, our local services seemed to be subject to frequent timetable changes; we tend to think this is only a modern phenomenon. In October 1906, the Windsor to Ascot service was cut back to five journeys on weekdays, the first being at 9.00a.m., and the same number on Sundays, the first being at 10.25 a.m. The route from Farnham Common to Slough also had five journeys on weekdays, also starting at 9.00 a.m., but only two on Sundays. Once again it can be noted that there were no early journeys for workmen.

There was a continuing undercurrent of criticism about the motor car even though the volume of such vehicles was derisory by today's standards. A traffic census taken at Maidenhead town hall on a normal July Sunday had revealed that 53 cars passed per hour, presumably in both directions combined; another check, taken at the same point on the Henley Regatta Sunday, had shown almost exactly twice as many cars per hour, over a 12 hour period. There were repeated calls in every edition of the local papers to reduce the speed limit from 20 to 15 miles per hour, with 12 in towns and on dangerous bends.

18) A charabanc licensed in 1904 standing outside Slough station, being used for a day's outing.

The year 1906 finished off with various reports on the G.W.R. bus services. Firstly, they were proposing to put up roadside timetables at Stoke Poges similar to those between Slough and Farnham Common and between Windsor and Ascot - there were probably no vandals to deface them in those days or if there were, they were actually punished. Secondly, fares were being reduced to 2 old pence between Farnham Common and the Yew Tree in one direction and Farnham Royal in the other and lastly, the parcels office in Farnham Common could now accept parcels for delivery all over the country, the parcels presumably getting into the system on one of the local buses bound for Slough.

And finally, the local paper reminded its readers that if they were asked to sign the petition currently circulating around Gerrards Cross for the G.W.R. to initiate a bus service from there to Uxbridge, they should remember that Gerrards Cross would only become prosperous if all its inhabitants - there were 417 people on the electoral register - spent all their money there!

CHAPTER 5

The continuing predominance of horse-drawn vehicles at the beginning of 1907 was borne out by a short item in one of the January editions of the local paper. It contained a report on a horse-drawn omnibus service which was then in operation between Gerrards Cross station, Chalfont St. Peter and Chalfont St. Giles. It was noted that the operator was a Mr S Crane and that the principal stopping place in both the Chalfonts was their respective post offices. Although the actual timings of the service were not given, there were apparently three journeys daily in each direction, one in the morning, one in the afternoon and one in the evening. In spite of the G.W.R. petition referred to in the previous Chapter, Gerrards Cross still had no motor bus service at that time, nor would it have until after the first world war.

The motor car however *was* beginning to be more popular, to the point where it was apparently starting to have an adverse impact on the numbers of bus users. That at least was what shareholders of the G.W.R. were told at their 1907 Annual General Meeting, but I find this difficult to believe and it is not borne out by the apparent popularity of the new motorised bus services. It is true to say that the G.W.R. was at least partially serving a particular class of passenger, namely those who were using the bus to access the railway network; this category of person could probably afford as an alternative, the relatively high cost of a motor car. If such people really did constitute the majority of bus passengers, it would also explain why the bus operators did not seem to go out of their way to transport labourers to their place of work first thing in the morning; nor did they hesitate to cut back their operations when the condition of the roads deteriorated in the winter months, again suggesting the non-routine character of the bus user.

Incidentally, it was also reported at the G.W.R. shareholders' meeting that the company's weekly wage bill averaged out at thirty five shillings per employee, or £1.75 in current money.

In February 1907, it was announced that the luxurious road motor attached to the Slough depot, referred to previously, was available for hire, for weddings for example. The paper reported that it had already been on hire to several Lords and the Royal Household, but it did not mention that it and the other new vehicles now being delivered were illuminated by electric lamps.

FARNHAM COMMON.

THE SLOUGH OBSERVER may be obtained of Messrs. Spong and Purser, Farnham Common.

READERS will find that ALBERT COX, Jobbing Gardener, Farnham Common, will do their work thoroughly and at moderate prices.

FARNHAM COMMON is probably the greatest source of patronage of the G.W.R. motor cars running between Slough and Beaconsfield. The cars have been on this route for a long time now, and, as it is one of the most perilous upon which the Company run cars, the fact that there has been no really serious accident speaks volumes for the care the drivers bestow on their work. Probably the best known of them is Driver Hayward, who has taken his car up and down the steep declivities between Slough and Beaconsfield, including the dangerous Dawney Bottom, for a considerable period without accident. Hayward has the reputation of being one of the most courteous, careful, and skilful drivers, and he can get as much work out a car as anybody.

Every Housewife likes Value for Money.

JOSEPH SPURGE,
GENERAL SUPPLY STORES,
FARNHAM COMMON,
MEETS THEIR REQUIREMENTS.
Specials just now—Grand Range of Calicos.

19) - Farnham Common Village News in 16th February 1907 edition of the Slough Observer. The G.W.R. bus driver who is mentioned was almost certainly the same Mr Hayward who was to appear in 1908 in a more enterprising role.

Also, that month, the Slough Observer reminded its readers of the parcel facility which was available between Farnham Common and Slough; up to 7lbs in weight could be carried for 2d. rising up in 1d. stages to 112 lbs for 6d. In the same edition of the paper, Mr Joseph Spurge, who kept the general stores in Farnham Common, at the corner of Victoria Road, was also reminding readers that he accepted parcels for carriage by train to any G.W.R. station in the country. Meanwhile in March, the 8d. fare from Slough was extended as far north as Hedgerley Corner, further substantial reductions being obtainable by buying books of 100 tickets. It is remarkable that at a time when the general population was much less mobile than it is today, there were sufficient people travelling regularly enough to justify introducing such a facility. It is also a contradiction of the earlier thoughts on who exactly was using the buses.

Exceptionally, there was a report on a horse bus service which linked Stoke Poges and Slough. This was provided by a wagonette operated by a Mr Glennerster which actually started from Hedgerley where the proprietor lived; this village was not yet served by motor bus, nor would it be until 1927. The wagonette came up the steep hill from the village and along the flat as far as the One Pin; there it joined the G.W.R. motor bus service, past the Fox and Pheasant, over Stoke Common and down Bells Hill and eventually into Slough where it then terminated at the station. It was making two trips each way each day which were in addition to the four journeys by G.W.R. road motors from Stoke Poges at 9.05 a.m, 2.00 p.m., 2.55 p.m. and 6.35 p.m.

There were frequent references in the papers to the fares on the G.W.R. buses around this time. Examples quoted included:

Farnham Common (Spurge's Corner) to Farnham Royal	2d.
Farnham Common (Spurge's Corner) to Hedgerley Corner	1d.
Windsor station to Eton Laundry or Chalvey Fields	2d.
Slough station to The Prince of Wales, Chalvey	1d.
Slough station to Farnburn Avenue, Slough	3d.

The following paragraph appeared in 2nd March 1907 edition of the local paper:

"The Great Western Railway Company are booming Farnham Common just now in a pamphlet entitled "Beechy Bucks, an Ideal Residential Centre." Among the information given is the fact that cheap return half-day tickets between Slough and Paddington are to be obtained on Wednesdays and Saturdays by trains running in connection with the 12.35 and 2.45 p.m. cars from Farnham Common on production of the road motor tickets at the booking office."

I wonder whether these tickets were specially stamped for subsequent identification by the ticket clerk at Slough station or were people more trustworthy in those days!

The 11th May 1907 edition of the Slough Observer reported on the annual burgeoning of bus services at the start of another summer. The Windsor to Ascot service was to have six trips in both directions, every day except Sunday when there were to be four. The Farnham

Common route to Slough, which was obviously very popular, was to have seven journeys each weekday, the first at 8.35 a.m. via Salt Hill and the second at 9.00 a.m. via Stoke Poges.

There were other reports during the summer of 1907 which were germane to our subject. The Slough Borough Council surveyor reported soon after the 4th of June that the portion of the road to Windsor which was oil tarred had been given a second dressing; this had resulted in the heavy traffic to and from Eton College on their famous speech day 'failing to raise any dust'. A month later, it was noted that the Burnham Beeches Estate Company were now providing a waiting room at Farnham Common in connection with the G.W.R. motor car service; since this service did not actually serve the Beeches until 1908, the facility was presumably in the village, although this was not stated. The G.W.R. did not open their own waiting room and parcels receiving office in the Broadway, Farnham Common until at least 1911. The fact the 1907 facility was a waiting room and not merely a shelter is interesting. I could find no reference to it in the minutes of the relevant Corporation of London committee and imagine that the Estate Company was probably a local property developer.

In August, the paper noted that there were now ample means to get from Slough to Windsor by pubic transport particularly between 1.45 and 2.15 every weekday afternoon; there were 2 trains, 2 buses and a horse-drawn brake. 'Needless to say' the paper said 'the whole lot are not always crowded'. At that time, the readers of the papers could hardly imagine the frequency of bus services between the two towns which was to build up in the early 1930's to the point where there was a bus every 2 to 3 minutes.

20) - Letter in 30th March 1907 edition of the Slough Observer regarding proposed station at Chalvey; the last two paragraphs are illuminating.

Twelve days after it actually happened, 12th October 1907 edition of the Slough Observer reported that the buses to Beaconsfield had now been taken off the portion of the route beyond Hedgerley Corner for the winter months. This was, as noted earlier, the beginning of the end of the Beaconsfield route for quite a long time, and it was undoubtedly caused by the opening of the new railway line from that town to London; this must have made rattling all the way to Slough before being able to board a London train somewhat less attractive. The remaining Farnham Common to Slough service was clearly well established however and it was reported that any letters handed in by 2.30 p.m. on a weekday - presumably at Mr Spurge's parcels office - would be taken by the 2.45 p.m. bus to Slough and delivered to addresses in London *the same day.* Have we really progressed? It was of course, the virtual absence of telephones (the names and numbers of new subscribers were actually listed regularly in the paper, by village) which presumably created the demand for such a service. There was however no mention of a supplementary charge for this express postal delivery.

Another interesting little aside in one of the October papers commented that those in Slough who were disappointed by the non-arrival of the electric trams, might like to take note of the fact that the price of properties in Teddington which **had** been reached by tram lines, had fallen significantly as a result, leading to many empty houses in that town.

During December 1907, there appeared the first of many references to a proposed highway from Hammersmith Broadway out to Slough and Windsor which apparently would be a sort of privately owned and regulated motorway with specific tolls for its usage. The number of intersections with other roads would, rather like a modern motorway, be limited. The interest for us is that it was proposed to incorporate a tramway. The whole project was to be the subject of The London and Windsor Motor Roads and Tramways Bill to be submitted to Parliament. During the next six months, the paper contained many reports on the progress or otherwise of the Bill and all the urban and district council meetings in the district devoted a lot of their time to objecting to it. Expert defence was organised (the LUT, interestingly, was one of the objectors) and as we know, the project, and others like it, as can be seen from the cutting on this page, never actually materialised. The idea of new private roads to rival the railways showed the far-sightedness of a few people; it is certain however that the motor car was total anathema for the majority of the population, at this time and for years to come. It was May 1908 before the various local councils were advised that the promoters had decided not to proceed with their ambitious scheme or schemes. The relief felt by all the different communities who would have been affected was clearly enormous. In the meanwhile, it has taken a further 90 years for the idea of privately owned and operated motorways to be seriously considered in this country.

21) - Report in 22nd February 1908 edition of the Slough Observer regarding two of the eventually abortive schemes to build privately owned motorways, incorporating tramways.

Reverting to actual events as opposed to grandiose plans, the G.W.R. responded to public demand towards the end of January 1908 by rerouting the buses returning to Slough from Windsor. Instead of darting back to the station down Mackenzie Street, they would now follow the route the outgoing buses had been using since the service started in 1904, that is to say straight down the High Street to Wexham Road and then back along Wellington Street. The paper commented that the new routeing would further popularise the 1d. fare from the Prince of Wales to the station; this was presumably another way of saying the passengers would get a longer ride for their money!

In the Slough Observer of 22nd February 1908, there was a tantalisingly brief report under the Farnham Royal village news which stated quite simply that "A motor bus is now running between Beaconsfield and Windsor". Nothing else was said in that or subsequent editions which at first sight seems surprising in view of the fact that motor bus developments were generally fairly widely reported. It is quite clear to my mind that the reason for this lack of interest stems from the fact that this service competed with the G.W.R. and was actually opposed by that company as we shall see in a moment; the newspaper in question was constantly supportive of that great enterprise, as were most of its readers, I get the impression. That said, it is very exciting indeed for bus researchers to think that as early as 1908, there was actually an independent motor bus operator in existence in the area.

What was apparently happening was that two men by the names of Hayward and Hill (one of them had almost certainly worked as a bus driver for the G.W.R. as the cutting on page 30 suggested), had gone into partnership and had purchased a second-hand double decker bus from a London dealer. They set out to run it in competition with the G.W.R. from Beaconsfield to Windsor, thus rather cleverly linking two of the existing G.W.R. services. The small print of the photograph on page 35 confirms both their names and the base of the enterprise as Beaconsfield. The Bucks Free Press which may have had no particular loyalty to the G.W.R. (as its name implies, it should not have had) in its 21st February 1908 edition, set out the full

22) - Report in 21st February 1908 edition of the Bucks Free Press incorporating the timetable for the Hayward and Hill bus service; in the first section, Beaconsfield railway station and the White Hart are transposed. Farnham Common cross-roads was where Victoria Road joined the Broadway, Kingsway coming out at that time right opposite.

timetable (see page 34). Unlike the G.W.R. service, it actually started at Beaconsfield station in the New Town before travelling up the hill to the White Hart in the Old Town, the northern terminus of the G.W.R. service. The report carried no mention of fares - perhaps they set out to undercut the railway company.

Unfortunately, the new initiative soon fell foul of its much larger competitor. Although there was no mention of it anywhere else in the paper, the following week's edition of the Bucks Free Press carried a letter from somebody signing himself as 'Well wisher' and disclaiming any financial interest in either the railway company or the upstart bus operator. He reported that the G.W.R. had forbidden access by the new bus to their station approaches at Beaconsfield and Slough, thus presumably denying it a lot of potential custom. The writer of the letter said that the new venture which was financially risky in any case, needed all the support it deserved, particularly from the railway company 'it is feeding'. It is clear that the station ban and perhaps other forms of restriction (could injunctions be obtained in those days for such matters?) led fairly quickly to the abandonment of that particular service on the part of Hayward and Hill.

23) - The bus operated by Messrs Hayward and Hill at the West Wycombe terminus of their second service, having been ousted from the first route.

Within six weeks of the initial report of their Windsor service, the Bucks Free Press stated that these two gentlemen had started at the beginning of April 1908 a service of motor buses (the plural is almost certainly not literal) between Beaconsfield and West Wycombe. This route was a long rambling ribbon of development with High Wycombe in the middle of it and it was crying out for a motor bus service; as we have already heard, the G.W.R. had been toying with covering a large part of this route in both 1904 and 1905 and to this day, it would be a wonderful candidate for a light rail operation. The report stated that the first bus left Beaconsfield at 10.30 in the morning except on Fridays, when it left at 9.30 for those attending market; there would be no Sunday service for the time being. Once again, there was no attempt to accommodate any working people who might have found the service useful first thing in the morning, but as commented on previously, people probably did not commute to work very much, or if they did, they could not afford the fares.

Since this service is outside the area of this publication, we will not pursue it. It was apparently taken over within 2 or 3 years by the Wycombe Livery and Haulage Company and the Beaconsfield end was cut back to Loudwater. The photo already referred to shows the bus parked at West Wycombe.

Reverting to our G.W.R. Farnham Common service, it was announced the first week in March 1908 that there was now an additional journey to Slough starting from Farnham Common at 7.50 in the morning - that was for white-collar workers almost certainly - and returning from Slough at 8.20. There must have been almost certainly one vehicle left overnight at the village terminus, probably in a pub yard - no vandals in those days!

By the middle of April, the G.W.R. had started 'circular motor trips embracing Burnham Beeches, Farnham Common and Stoke Poges on Tuesdays'. They probably employed the luxurious saloon referred to earlier on these tourist journeys, but there was no mention of frequency or other details; a few weeks later the circular trip ticket was disclosed to be 1/4d. or 7 current pence.

At the end of April, it was reported that Mr Glennerster's bus - the use of that word is interesting - would resume running twice a day during the summer months between Hedgerley and the Reindeer Inn in Slough (The Old Reindeer stood on the north side of the High Street and had an archway entrance into its back yard; it was pulled down in the 1930's). Once again, I find the seasonal nature of these stage carriage services as opposed to summer outings quite curious. Naturally we all prefer to go out in 'nice' weather but surely many users of these services would have required the facility all the year round! The fares charged for these journeys were not cheap; Mr Glennerster apparently

HEDGERLEY.
DEATH OF MR. F. GLENNERSTER.

It is with sincere regret we have to announce the death of Mr. Frederick Glennerster, of Mount Pleasant, Hedgerley, the proprietor of the Slough and Hedgerley 'bus, which occurred after a short illness on Wednesday from heart failure. Deceased, who was 67 years of age, had resided at Hedgerley for 31 years last May, and had driven the 'bus to and from Slough for 11 or 12 years. He was widely known and greatly respected, his cheery disposition and obliging manner making him a general favourite. He was first and foremost in everything connected with the welfare of the village, and threw himself heart and soul into anything that he took up.

24) - Part of a report in 8th August 1908 edition of the Slough Observer covering the death of the proprietor of the Hedgerley horse bus.

charged a 1/- single or 2/- return to go on his bus from Hedgerley. 2/- would have bought ten pints of beer in those days, although beer was apparently a relatively cheap commodity!

The popularity of the G.W.R's service to Burnham Beeches for day trippers was not however in doubt because Luff's local rail and bus timetable, which incidentally was heavily advertised each week in their paper, apparently showed 13 trips a day to the Beeches as from the beginning of May. The paper never said in so many words that Burnham Beeches had now practically replaced Hedgerley Corner as the terminus of the journeys to Farnham Common, at any rate in the summer time; the change actually took place on 1st May 1908. The popularity of Burnham Beeches certainly knew no bounds because in that same month, it was reported that the inhabitants of Yiewsley and West Drayton (both of which are several miles nearer London than Slough) could now enjoy motor trips round the Beeches. As we shall see later, the London General were soon to exploit the attraction of this wonderful stretch of preserved common land as they were to do with Epping Forest to the east; in the meanwhile, the operator of the Yiewsley trips was not revealed.

Finally, in May 1908 the telephone reached Farnham Common.

The following month, the local paper reported that "the local Jehus" (a biblical reference to a gentleman called Jehu who had a reputation for driving his chariot at high speed) which presumably referred to all the horse-drawn vehicles either plying for hire or operating services, had done 'a roaring trade' over the Whitsun weekend. At the beginning of July, the GWR resumed running their motor buses through to Beaconsfield "for the summer months". In fact this resumption was limited to two journeys on Wednesdays and Saturdays only. It was also noted that the narrow road between Farnham Royal and Burnham Beeches (this was presumably Crown Lane), which was the usual route for the GWR buses to take to the latter place, needed to be widened. The G.W.R. replied to Council complaints that the road had been used "for many years" (an interesting thought) by brakes and omnibuses (presumably horse-drawn though not stated) coming from Slough and Amersham stations (the latter seems strange in view of the deviation it would have involved). The topic however preoccupied the local minds for some weeks; at the beginning of August, it was reported:

"The G.W.R. have promised to use small motor cars where possible and to reduce their service along this particular road but the large motor buses and charabancs from London and the suburbs cannot be prevented from using the road without an order from the Local Government Board which is difficult to obtain".

It appears that all this related to periodic G.W.R. excursions to the Beeches rather than their regular service which used the main road.

At around this time (Summer 1908), a traffic survey was carried out one Sunday along the Bath Road in Slough. It will be recalled that in Chapter 2, it was said that only 121 cars crossed Windsor bridge in 1904 in a whole week. By 1908, almost this same number (110 to be precise) came along the Bath Road in an hour and a quarter. This was always of course a main road, it was a Sunday and it was high summer, but the apparent increase is certainly striking.

The 10th October edition of the paper reported once more on the Slough and Hedgerley bus (presumably the wagonette). The service had somehow survived the passing of its original proprietor and the new management had decided to only discontinue its second journey during the winter months, starting on the following Monday. Presumably the remaining journey must have laid over at the Reindeer for quite some time to have made it worthwhile for anybody coming into town.

In November 1908, Slough Council considered at some length the level of noise which was being generated by the G.W.R's motor omnibuses. The following is an extract of the report on the debate (The bus referred to, No. 66, was a Milnes-Daimler; I understand this vehicle had a particularly noisy form of drive transmission):

> "The noise and other defects of the Great Western Railway Company's motor omnibuses seem to trouble many people living on the road between Slough and Windsor Stations. The matter came before the last meeting of the Slough Council, and now a number of Eton people have petitioned for the discontinuance of the vehicles. It is to be hoped, however, that the Company will consider the convenience of the general public and think twice before they take this step. The "Morning Post" says: "There are good grounds for the hope that the noise and other defects of the motor omnibus may soon be overcome, for it is worth the labours of mechanical science to improve a vehicle which has undoubtedly come to stay."

25) - Report in 5th December 1908 edition of the Slough Observer regarding the noise level of the G.W.R. motor buses.

"Mr Lidstone moved "That this council requests the Great Western Railway Company to take the necessary steps to lessen the noise produced by their motor omnibuses." He said that everybody sitting in the room knew the deafening noise made and anyone who had any clerical work to do must fully sympathise with the resolution. The noise at times was simply beyond endurance. It only needed a little more surveillance on the part of the people in charge of these machines to render them far less noisy. Mr Godfrey said "He suffered a very great deal from the nuisance. He thought it should be possible for the Great Western Railway Company to get rid of the trouble without much difficulty." The Great Western road motors were far and away the most noisy that passed through Slough so far as his experience went. On many occasions during the summer there had been a large number of London motor buses, half a dozen at a time, with big parties, through the town, and the noise they made was not more than an ordinary motor, which was quite enough for most mortals. The Great Western engineers should be able to find out the cause of the great noise made by their buses. There was one motor in particular he should like to see go into the Thames so long as no one was on it. It was a particularly bad one. The number was 66. The Council should approach the Great Western Railway Company in a friendly spirit and persuade them to "get rid" of what was a great nuisance to the public".

Thus 1908 came to a close with still only one motor bus operator in the area; the only other one which had dared to raise its head had been quickly seen off by the highly regarded but no doubt, at heart, ruthless G.W.R.

CHAPTER 6

By 1909, the novelty for the local population of the G.W.R. bus services was probably beginning to wear off because there were fewer reports in the local papers which are relevant to our story during that year or indeed 1910.

There were however two items in the Spring of 1909 which remind us of the general environment in which private motor cars were being enjoyed. The first referred to the question of the 10 mile an hour speed limit through Slough which everybody, except the motorists presumably, had been pressing for, for several months. The local paper noted that although this had come into effect on 1st May 1909, 'the gentry' (their words) were still ignoring the signs. If the gentry were the car owners, these cars would have replaced their private horse-drawn carriages so again, it is not entirely clear to me how the G.W.R. could be saying that the growth of the motor car was sapping the profitability of their bus services. The second road-related report stated that the road going north from Salt Hill (nowadays the A.355) had been tarred up as far as the Green Man, a pub which was there until very recently on the hill of that name between Farnham Royal and Farnham Common. It was reported that the Farnham Commoners were unanimous in wanting the road surfaced as far as their village; probably the story of the dust on the roadside strawberries was a factor in their thinking!

Reverting to public road transport, Burnham Parish Council expressed great dissatisfaction in May 1909 about the fact that there were not enough trains stopping at their station, known in those days as Burnham Beeches, on the G.W.R. main line to and from London. They went on to consider the possibility of initiating "a road service" (mode of traction not specified, but presumably motorised) to connect the village to the London and South

26 - G.W.R. bus, licensed AF 141 in July 1905, waiting in Slough station yard, en route to Stoke Poges golf club, as indicated by the board fixed on its side. Flexible destination blinds only appeared some 20 years later.

Western Railway terminus at Windsor (now Windsor Riverside). Given that this would have been in defiance of the G.W.R. who, to my knowledge, were the only motor bus owners in the district, one wonders who they thought would operate such a service. Alas, it was another idea which came to naught.

Whilst on the subject of Burnham Beeches station, it is somewhat surprising that the G.W.R. who, as we have already seen, appreciated the tourist potential of the Beeches as far back as the 1890's, never to my knowledge ran any horse-drawn service between that station and the place itself and a motorised connection for only a very short time in the late 1920's. The pre 1914-18 war guide books did point out to their readers that the Beeches should best be reached from Slough unless the visitor was fond of walking but the casual day-tripper might well have assumed that he should book through to the station which actually bore the name of Burnham Beeches. The absence of any link at least partially explains the infrequency of stopping trains which the Council were complaining about.

> "WHY DO NOT THE POLICE ENFORCE THE LIMIT?"
> TO THE EDITOR OF THE SLOUGH, ETON, AND WINDSOR OBSERVER.
>
> DEAR SIR,—Now that you have the 10 mile limit at Slough, I wonder why no notice is taken of the G.W.R. buses which constantly travel along the High-street at about 17 miles per hour and turn from the Windsor-road to the High-street in a reckless way. I myself was stopped only a few days ago and told that I was travelling too fast, although I had kept behind the bus all the way along the High-street. It is these heavy vehicles which damage the roads so much. . . . . Why do not the Police enforce the limit?
>
> Yours faithfully
> J. E. CASHNELLY.
> East Burnham Grove,
> Slough.
> Sept. 20th, 1909.

27 - Letter in 25th September 1909 edition of the Slough Observer regarding the apparently excessive speeds of the buses in Slough.

The G.W.R. did actually start a new bus service in our area in 1909 although it was not a real service in the fullest sense. In June that year, a splendid new golf course with residential accommodation was opened in the impressive mansion known as Stoke Park off Park Road, Stoke Poges. The house still fulfills the function of a golf club and a hotel today, but alas without a dedicated bus service. The opening in 1909 was a very prestigious event, attended by the grandest people from all over Europe, most of whom were listed in the local newspapers. Not wishing to be left out, the G.W.R. initiated a service from Slough station to the new club "to connect with principal trains". The local paper reported that the single fare was 6 pence each way, but whether the service was actually available to the general public to and from intermediate points was not made clear; since so little was made of it, I suspect it was not. That said however, the service continued to be operated by the G.W.R. until July 1915 when the war killed it off. They actually started the service again in the 1920's and a Windsor based independent operator, Robert Last, operated a service to the club in the early 1930's before it was taken over by London Transport.

Reverting to the early days of the service, I assume that the G.W.R. bus illustrated on page 39 actually went up the ¾ mile drive to the big house to deliver its enthusiastic passengers to their destination. The present management of the club kindly allowed me to peruse the minute book from the inception of the establishment but there was no mention of the bus service. This surely means that the route must have been an entirely arms-length commercial operation for the G.W.R; not **all** the gentry had motor cars!

The Slough Observer was very happy to report at about the same time as the opening of Stoke Park, that the G.W.R. had at last revised the fare structure of the Slough to Windsor service by breaking it down into three 1d bites; this was something the paper had been pressing for some time. The first 1d took the traveller starting at Slough Station as far out of town as the Prince of Wales (again, a pub of that name there until very recently). The second tranche went through to Eton College and the last 1d. took passengers over the river and up Thames Street to the G.W.R. station, now known as Windsor Central.

There was another report early in the year which also related to fares. The same paper which welcomed the simplification of the Slough/Windsor fares also suggested to the G.W.R. that the 4d. return tickets being issued on the trains - what a bargain; less than 2 new pence there and back - between the two towns should become interchangeable with the buses. In fact, they said that the return halves of both railway and omnibus tickets should be available by either road or rail. Apparently, the G.W.R. had started 1909 by honouring the London and South Western Railway return halves from London Waterloo to Windsor Riverside so it seemed a short step to make their own local service interchangeable. The report ended by saying: "Of course, all return tickets on the motor cars would be subject to there being room on the cars". However earnestly the proposal was argued, it fell on deaf ears until such time as competition appeared in 1912.

In 1909 and in the years which preceded it, there were fairly regular reports on the amounts which had been spent by the G.W.R. on plans for a new railway line from Windsor to Ascot. In August that year, for example, it was noted that some £83,000 had already been expended (this would have been a very sizeable sum in money of the day); the report stated, quite self evidently, that the opening of the line would spell the death-knell for the bus service. As we know, the line was never built and we have already learned that the G.W.R. buses continued operating on the Ascot route right through until 1931. In the meanwhile, similar reports about the proposed railway line continued until 23rd December 1911 edition of the Slough Observer when it was announced that the powers given to the G.W.R. by Act of Parliament in 1904 would no longer be exercised and the plan would be withdrawn. Windsor Council were not amused and even tried unsuccessfully to persuade the G.W.R. to pay for a new footbridge over the existing line as a form of consolation for the considerable disappointment felt in the locality.

The owners of the armies of charabancs which used to descend on Windsor on Ascot race days to pick up the punters at the Central Station would not have been sorry however. The G.W.R. themselves developed a regular trade up until the start of the first World War, charging the princely sum of 3/- (15 current pence) for a return trip to Ascot racecourse from the Royal Borough.

1909 was the year in which the Road Fund started. For the first time, the owners of motor vehicles had to pay to put their fearsome monsters on the King's Highway although since 1904, they had been required to pay both a small fee (£1) to initially register their vehicle and obtain a licence plate for it and 5/- (25 pence) for their driver's licence. The new tax on the vehicle itself which, as today was an annual one, ranged from £2.2.0 on low horsepower cars up to £21 on those over 40 horsepower. A tax of 3 old pence was also introduced on each gallon of petrol.

The noisy motor bus was not having it all its own way, even as late as 1909. There was a magazine circulating at the time called "The Road" which amongst other things reported stage coach services. During the summer of that year, it noted that The Magnet had "started its season" early in June, running three days a week between Great Missenden and Chenies, serving the town of Amersham and the Metropolitan Railway station at Chalfont Road (later named Chalfont & Latimer). Apparently, the coach left Missenden at 2.30p.m. on Mondays, Wednesdays and Saturdays and returned from Chenies at 5 o'clock, the journey taking 1 hour and 20 minutes each way. The single fare was 3/- (15 pence) and the return fare 5/-; "box seat 1/- (5 pence) extra each way". The journey was described as a most enjoyable drive through charming country and the coach was reported as "well horsed". The fares were actually quite expensive and the whole venture was most likely regarded as an outing rather than as a means of getting from A to B, but fascinating nonetheless.

To conclude the year 1909, the text of a letter written to the Slough Observer on 19th October that year by somebody signing himself Fair Play is partially reproduced below. It touches on several interesting strands which seemed to constantly recur in the public debate at that time about the pros and cons of public transport between the two towns which are the subject of this publication.

"Sir, I see that the Slough Council propose to consider the question of petitioning the Great Western Railway Company to erect a halt at Chalvey Bridge. When the matter comes before the council I hope that they will consider it in all its bearings. If there is a large number of working men in Chalvey employed in Windsor, it is the duty of the council to do all they can for them, but I am under the impression that most of the Chalvey working men employed outside Slough are employed at Eton, and surely they don't want to go to Windsor to get to Eton. What then would be the chief value of a halt at Chalvey Bridge? Would it not encourage Chalvey people to shop at Windsor instead of Slough? I am afraid it would, and that consequently it would do harm to Slough. Trade has been very bad in Slough for some years past, and it is bad now. Slough tradesmen have been very hard hit by the motor buses running to Windsor, and any increase in the facilities for getting to the Royal Borough would only hit them harder. Do they deserve such treatment? I don't think they do. When people make up their minds to have a motor ride they don't consider whether they can buy the article they want in Slough as cheaply as in Windsor. They really go to Windsor because they want the ride. Slough council must not forget that Chalvey working men can now ride from "The Prince of Wales" to Eton by motor bus for a penny, and they can go right up to the G.W.R. Station at Windsor for twopence. I shall no doubt be told that the motor buses do not start from Slough early enough. Well, if a party of working men would undertake to go from "The Prince of Wales" to Windsor at a definite time every morning no doubt the G.W.R. Company would run a bus or even two especially for them. The council must not forget that they represent all classes and that the tradesmen are entitled to some consideration."

Easter 1910, which came at the end of March that year, was apparently nice and sunny and the streets of both Slough and Windsor had to be frequently watered to lay the dust. As previously mentioned, there was and had been for some years, a constant underlying current of deep-felt concern about the road dust menace. It was frequently said by various correspondents, both expert and lay, that there was no more prolific a source of disease than the dust generated by passing motor vehicles. Surely this must have been a form of paranoia resulting from a lack of familiarity with the new fangled internal combustion engine.

28 - G.W.R. bus DA 118 on the service from Slough to Burnham Beeches, via Salt Hill and Farnham Common.

Meanwhile, on Good Friday and Easter Monday (not on the Sabbath) an "observation car" ran from Slough Station on a picturesque tour of South Bucks. The passengers went to Burnham Beeches, Beaconsfield (I understand that in the 1920's, lunch was usually taken on this tour at the Saracens Head), Jordans and Chalfont St Giles before returning through Gerrards Cross and over Stoke Common. The fare was 3/6 (17½ new pence), provided a minimum of 8 passengers turned up to book. This tour appears to have been a considerable extension of the circular motor trips which the G.W.R. had started in April 1908 for the summer of that year, referred to in the previous chapter. Meanwhile, for those who did not want to go on the tour, the regular bus service between Windsor and Slough was supplemented on the Easter Monday so as to provide a half-hourly frequency.

By the Autumn of 1910, it was being reported that the G.W.R. motor buses returning to Slough from Windsor were usually running empty after passing the top of Mackenzie Street so the loop back to the station which had been introduced in response to public demand at the beginning of 1908 was, clearly, not being widely used. It remained the route however until the service was withdrawn at the end of July 1913 (of which, more anon).

Even in those early days when Councils could actually afford to pay for things, they were not sympathetic to the bus user; at the end of 1910, a request to Stoke Poges Council to put up a seat at The Pound for the benefit of bus users at that stop was given the thumbs down.

The G.W.R's own magazine published some data in the Autumn of 1910 which related to a week in June that year. Apparently, some 56% of the 952 passengers who rode on the motor buses from Farnham Common to Slough in that week (over 130 a day, including Sundays) went on to travel somewhere by train from Slough. The parcels were even more adventurous; 92% of the 25 carried that week on the buses continued on by rail to another destination.

The year 1911 was also a quiet year in terms of motor bus service developments. Not far away from our area however, Maidenhead started to enjoy its first such service in June that year. Routes were launched by the G.W.R. from the station there to Hurley and to Taplow respectively. Within a few days of their inception, the Maidenhead Advertiser reported as follows: "The G.W.R. have at last put on a motor service to and from Maidenhead station. It will now be possible to get to The Thicket, Littlewick Green and Hurley for a few pence at fixed hours. We would welcome something from Boulters or Maidenhead Court; however we accept with gratitude. The line of buses over the bridge from Taplow and Maidenhead stations .... is good for the steamers".

At about the same time as this was happening, the Slough Observer reported that an additional "late car" had been put on the Slough/Windsor service on Wednesday and Saturday nights leaving Slough at 10.00 p.m. and returning from Windsor at 10.30 p.m. or the end of the performance at the Theatre Royal, whichever was the later. The midweek early closing culture determined that Wednesday was the obvious complement to Saturday for an evening out. In today's society, Friday would probably be the second busiest evening. Sundays however must also have been popular because the local paper was suggesting that the G.W.R. should run "two motor omnibuses" at nine o'clock in the evening from Slough; "Last Sunday, the motor was packed before it reached The Prince of Wales and about a dozen passengers were left behind".

Reverting for a moment to February 1911, the Slough Observer, still faithfully supportive of the G.W.R., reported that that company had placed an order with Dennis Brothers of Guildford (still major bus builders to this day) for 10 more buses. Apparently, they were to be smaller than the existing "standard design" and more economical to operate; on the other hand, they were to be "of higher speed" and almost certainly single-decker since they were expected to be used on country routes where traffic was light.

The dreaded motor car was gaining popularity at a phenomenal pace. The number of cars licensed nationally in 1911 reached 75,600, compared with only 53,200 the previous year. This represented an increase of no less than 42%, but it still only amounted to one third of one per cent of the total number on the road today. At a local level, The Car magazine, whose editor, the then Lord Montagu, lived at Ditton Park, Slough, reported that at the end of 1910, there were 715 cars licensed in Buckinghamshire and 1,100 in Berkshire. The Slough based G.W.R. motor bus fleet at that time, although not all originally licensed in Bucks, represented numerically a significant percentage of the grand total of 26 heavy motor vehicles licensed in the County.

☞ COUNTRY RESIDENTS SEE PAGE ONE.

JUNE, 1911.
TIME TABLE
OF
RAILWAY, MOTOR and OMNIBUS SERVICES
To and from SLOUGH.

.. Issued by ..
Headington & Son
BY APPOINTMENT

Forage Merchants to H.M. the King.
CORN, CAKE & SEED MERCHANTS,
COAL & COKE FACTORS,
77, High Street, & Mackenzie Street

Mills & Granaries:	Coal Wharf:
CHURCH STREET,	G.W.R. STATION,

SLOUGH.
Telephone 044. Telegrams: Headington, Slough.

Ent. at Stationers Hall.   PRICE ONE PENNY.

SLOUGH, ETON and WINDSOR MOTOR BUS.
Fares: between Slough & Eton 2d., Slough & Windsor 3d.
From Slough Station (via High Street), Week Days.—
8.30 9.30 10.30 11.30 12.30 2.0 3.0 4.0 4.30 5.0 6.0 7.0
8.0 9.0 *10.0
* Wednesdays and Saturdays only

Sundays.—1.15 2.0 3.0 4.0 5.0 6.0 7.0 8.0 9.0

From Windsor.—Week Days.—9.0 10.0 11.0 12.0 1.0
2.30 3.30 4.30 5.30 6.30 7.0 7.30 8.30 9.30 *10.30
* Wednesdays and Saturdays only

Sundays.—2.20 3.30 4.30 5.30 6.30 7.30 8.30 8.45 9.30

SLOUGH, STOKE and HEDGERLEY BRAKE.
| From Hedgerley | 9.25 | *2.45 |
| " Slough | 1.10 | *8.10 |

* Saturdays only.
Fares: Stoke 6d.; Hedgerley 1/-

Worth Remembering !!!
All our Goods at Store Prices, and we give 2½ per cent. Rebate for Cash.

HEADINGTON & SON,
Seedsmen, Corn and Flour Merchants,

High St., and Mackenzie St., Slough.

Established 1840.   Telephone 041.

GRIFFITH & WALDEN

Chemists and Pharmacists,

HIGH STREET, SLOUGH.

Tonic Neuralgic Mixture

An Entirely New and Infallible
.. Remedy for ..

NEURALGIA and all other Nerve Complaints.

It gives Speedy Relief.	It is good for Nervous Headache
It is a Tonic.	
It strengthens the Nerves	It gives tone to the Digestive Organs.
It invigorates the system	
It gives Rest and Sleep at Night.	It has a steadily increasing Sale.
It cures where other Medicine fails.	It is the Cure for Neuralgia, no matter how violent.
It removes the Pain.	

Sold in Bottles at 1/6 each.

MOTOR OMNIBUS SERVICE.
Slough, Stoke, Farnham & the Beeches.

Slough	...	825	9 55	1150	115	315	535	7 5	...	...	...
Stoke Green	...	...	10 0	1155	120	320	540	710	...	...	...
Stoke Church	...	...	10 5	12 0	125	325	545	715	...	...	...
Farnham Royal	845	1015	1210	135	335	555	725	...	...	...	
Farnham Com.	850	1020	1215	140	340	6 0	730	...	...	...	
B. Beeches	...	...	1220	...	350	615	740	...	...	...	
B. Beeches	...	...	1225	...	355	620	745	...	...	...	
Farnham Com.	9 3	1032	1227	147	357	622	752	...	...	...	
Farnham Royal	910	1035	1230	150	4 0	625	755	...	...	...	
Stoke Church	920	1045	1240	...	410	635	8 5	...	...	...	
Stoke Green	925	1050	1245	...	115	640	810	...	...	...	
Slough	935	11 0	1255	215	125	650	820	...	...	...	

Sundays.

Slough Station	...	10 50	2 0	3 25	6 5	...	...
Farnham Royal	...	11 10	2 20	3 45	6 25	...	...
Farnham Common	...	11 15	2 30	3 50	6 30	...	...
Burnham Beeches	...	11 20	2 30	3 56	6 35	...	...
Burnham Beeches	...	11 25	2 35	4 0	7 20	...	...
Farnham Common	...	11 30	2 40	4 5	7 25	...	...
Farnham Royal	...	11 35	2 45	4 10	7 30	...	...
Slough Station	...	12 0	3 10	4 35	7 50	...	...

Slough Station & Stoke Poges Golf Club.
Week Days.

Slough Station	10 30	†11 15	12 35	3 55	†4 55	6†10	...	...
Golf Club	10 40	11 25	12 45	4 5	5 5	6 20	...	...
Golf Club	10 50	†11 35	12 50	†2 05	10	†6 40	...	...
Slough Station	11 5	11 50	1 5	4 35	5 25	6 55	...	...

Sundays.

Slough Station	9 25	10 35	11 15	4 30	5 40	...	...	...
Golf Club	9 35	10 45	11 25	4 40	5 50	...	...	...
Golf Club	...	9 45	10 55	11 50	5 20	6 5	...	...
Slough Station	10 0	11 10	13 5	5 35	6 20	...	...	...

† Will only run if sufficient passengers (minimum of 4).

---

29 - Extracts relating to bus services from the Headington & Sons June 1911 timetable for Slough; three of the services are motorised and one horse-drawn.

On page 45, there are reproduced the parts of Headington & Sons' Slough timetable for June 1911 which relate to bus services. As can be seen from the extract, Headingtons were apparently forage merchants by appointment to His Majesty the King so why they chose to publish a transport timetable is not obvious. That said, there are no particular surprises in the timetable, for those who have remained faithful to this narrative so far. The only non-motorised service which was included was the Hedgerley brake; it now had a second journey on Saturdays only, but the fare was still 1/- (5 pence) single. Incidentally, its departure point in Slough is not specified. Why were the other horse-bus services, which surely must have still existed, not mentioned? There were no motor buses between Slough and Windsor on Sunday mornings, but there was one journey to Burnham Beeches, presumably for the heathen Londoners and three journeys to Stoke Poges Golf Club for the even more sinful golfers. The other interesting aspect of the Golf Club route is that three of the weekday journeys only operated if at least four people showed up. What happened to the would be passengers waiting at the other end who might be quite numerous, if the outgoing journey did not run?

There was a rail strike in August 1911 and this appeared to divide the local populace into one of two camps. The Observer, being very pro-G.W.R., supported those brave souls who went on working; this group included the motor bus drivers and conductors who may have been on different rates of pay which were not in contention. The other camp condemned the scabs, as we would call them today, but in spite of that the bus workers were rewarded by a large increase in the number of their passengers who apparently abandoned the skeleton rail services at Slough and continued their journey home to Windsor on one of the buses, which may or may not have been supplemented. There was no actual mention of railway season tickets being usable on the bus services.

30 - G.W.R. bus AF 684, parked facing south on the wrong side of the road, outside the Company's waiting room and parcels receiving office in the Broadway, Farnham Common; the parade of shops is still there today virtually unchanged. The photo is no earlier than the second half of 1911.

The majority of bus services in inner London during the period covered by this book were horse-drawn and some of these lasted up to August 1914 when the Army commandeered the horses. The motor bus however not only became more and more prevalent during the first decade of the century, but developed its speed and reliability. The point was reached when the London General Omnibus Company (the 'General'), which had been formed in 1908 out of a merger of several operators in the inner London area, was eyeing the possibility of using their considerable fleet of double deckers which were largely unused on Sundays, to transport people out of town on their day of rest (Saturday was still a working day for most). The destinations for these country services, and we must remember that London did not stretch out so far in those days, would be historic towns such as St. Albans and Windsor, and beauty spots within the same, say, 25 mile radius such as Epping Forest, the Surrey Hills and Burnham Beeches. Return journeys of this distance, using the outer end of the underground lines as a starting point for the buses, were increasingly viable for bus operators; the General had been taken over by the Underground Company at the beginning of 1912.

Journeys of such a length were also able to be contemplated by the general populace in the immediate pre-war years and after the end of hostilities during the 1920's. By the thirties, a different type of trade had developed; by then, comfortable motor coaches could easily encompass a day's trip as far as the south coast and the popularity of the slower stopping bus services to the intermediate points such as the Beeches slowly declined.

All this is by way of general background to the developments which began in 1912 and which were to transform the bus scene in Slough and Windsor and provide the G.W.R. with some serious opposition both as regards frequency and level of fares.

Chapter 7

As hinted at in the last chapter, 1912 marked the coming of something of a revolution in terms of the number of motor buses operating in and around Slough and Windsor. The G.W.R., still the only local operator at the start of that year, was to be shaken out of its unchallenged, possibly complacent, position, by the arrival of the London General Omnibus Company which already, at that time, had over 2,000 motor buses on the road as against just over a hundred for the G.W.R. over the whole of their area.

The original reason why our two towns had enjoyed motor buses as early as the first years of the century - as already said, it really was very early by national standards - was that Slough was a major stopping point on a railway system the owners of which, of all the railway companies, were determined to develop feeder bus services. It also had a practical advantage as an operating base in having the road motor workshops for the whole of the G.W.R. fleet in the town.

The reason for the General invasion was altogether different. It was a combination of the relative proximity to London of the area - a feasible day trip - and the fact that it contained, and still does, three major, what we would now call tourist attractions, in the shape of Windsor Castle, the River Thames and Burnham Beeches. Having said that, the General quickly saw the potential for local bus services in the area as we shall see, but to my mind, it is clear that the original catalyst for them was the possibility of turning a part of their vast fleet to good account on Sundays by serving the attractions just mentioned.

Another longer term result of the invasion from the east was the fact that the two towns with their north/south road link through Eton formed the effective western

LONDON TO WINDSOR.

FOR A SHILLING.

The London General Omnibus Co. are extending their service further and furthere afield.

Within a day or two a new service to Staines from Hounslow Barracks Station will be started. It will go via Feltham, Bedfont and Ashford, the cost of the journey being fourpence.

On Sundays another route has been selected which will undoubtedly prove extremely popular. With Hounslow Barracks Station still as a base, the omnibuses will run to Harlington Corner, thence to Colnbrook and Slough,

ON TO WINDSOR.

The passenger is taken through some very pretty country, and, granted fine weather, the journey will be one of the most pleasant out of London.'

The fare from Hounslow to Windsor is to be sixpence, and as it only costs another sixpence to go from the Mansion House to Hounslow the double fare of a shilling from the heart of the City to the Royal borough is not a bad investment.

The company's new motor-'buses of the light type will be utilised for this service.

31 - Report in 12th July 1912 edition of the Slough Chronicle covering the start of the L.G.O.C. Hounslow to Windsor service.

boundary of the London Transport statutory operating area when it was created in 1933. (Even Ledgers Road, Chalvey was outside the area although it was only a quarter of a mile to the west of the main road). In time, this meant that right up to the 1970's when the route pattern was finally analysed and amended in a bus passenger marketing survey, the centre of Slough was the boundary between the two main operators, London Transport and Thames Valley. The practical effect of this was that the pattern of services was essentially north/south, the result being that it was not possible until the 1970's to get a direct bus from Cippenham to Langley for example, or from Maidenhead to other points east of Slough.

The year 1912 started quietly enough with a report in February of a near accident to a G.W.R. bus being driven from Slough to Windsor. It was apparently proceeding about its lawful occasions approaching Eton, near Willow Brook, which to this day is a cul-de-sac on the right hand side going south, when it was overtaken by a motor car belonging to the Bucks and Berks Motor Company. The car cut in too sharply and clipped the offside front wheel of the bus. The bus driver lost control and the vehicle swerved to the near side and through the fence into Agar's Plough. Fortunately, nobody was injured and the damage to the bus was limited to the steering gear being put out of action. It is somewhat amazing however that with so few vehicles on the road, two of them needed to collide at all.

MOTOR 'BUSES TO WINDSOR.

WEEK-DAY SERVICE TO RUN.

On Sunday last a special motor omnibus service from Hounslow to Windsor was inaugurated, the route taken being via Bath-road, Harlington, Colnbrook, Slough, and Eton. There were half-hour services, and the 'buses were crowded throughout the day. The total number of passengers conveyed was 4,357. The fare from Hounslow to Windsor is 6d., and it is now possible for a person to travel from the Mansion House via Hounslow to Windsor for 1s. Windsor people can also make the journey to London for one shilling. The service is now doubled, and on Saturday a week-day service is to run every hour from Hounslow to Windsor, starting at nine o'clock. It will bring a great many people into the town, and it must be good for the Windsor shopkeepers. Some of the London papers describe the service as "Sundays at Beautiful Windsor."

32 - Report in 20th July 1912 edition of the Windsor Express, again covering the new L.G.O.C. Windsor service.

Meanwhile in their July 1912 leaflet (the leaflets came out monthly in the four years up to the war), which would have been published at the end of the previous month, the General announced that a new service, numbered 62, would be started shortly on Sundays only between Hounslow Barracks (now Hounslow West) underground station and Windsor Castle, passing through Colnbrook, Langley, Slough and Eton. After an interval of seven years, Colnbrook was again to be linked to the outside world by a motor bus service. The minimum fare was to be a penny and the maximum sixpence; this was extremely good value by G.W.R. standards, considering that the journey time proved to be 70 minutes. Whilst on the subject of fares, the charge from the William IV at Langley, which is the nearest the service got to that community, to Windsor Market Hall, as the Guildhall was then known, was 3d; compare that to the G.W.R. fares.

Sure enough, on 14th July, the service commenced on Sundays only, as route 62. Unlike the G.W.R. who never got around to it, the General had introduced numbers for their services in November 1908. The Slough Chronicle two days before the service started opined that the route 'will understandably prove extremely popular' (they were absolutely right in that) and it went on to say that 'granted fine weather, the journey will be one of the most pleasant out of London'. The reference to fine weather was far more pertinent than it would be today, travelling as we now can in warm and cosy buses. The vehicles used on the 62 and all the services we shall be reading about, were 34-seater 'B' Class double-deckers which, like the G.W.R. double-deckers, were open to the four winds of heaven, to say nothing of torrential rain. The 16 slatted wooden seats on the top deck or the 'outside' did have waterproof covers to unroll over the passengers' laps, but the top half of the travellers was very exposed. At least people were sensible enough to wear hats in those days; why that habit has disappeared, I shall never know. Although closed top double-deckers started to appear in central London in 1925, it was the start of the 1930's before they could be found in the outer areas such as Slough and Windsor, by which time I should think the general populace had developed an immunity to the perils of riding on the top deck. The drivers did not fare any better, there being no windscreens or cabs until the end of the 1920's but at least they were provided with waterproof clothing. Having said all that, the General certainly did not hide the fact that their buses were exposed on the top deck. Their monthly leaflets up to the war carried the slogan 'Open Air to Everywhere'.

33 - The top deck of an L.G.O.C. double-decker bus; the waterproof covers can be seen attached to the offside row of seats.

When the service first started, the buses operating it came from the General's Turnham Green garage as the Hounslow garage was yet to be opened. This meant that at the start and end of the day, the buses had to travel empty for some 5 miles without carrying any passengers and it also meant that this route, and another one to Staines, was completely detached from the rest of the London bus network.

Interestingly enough, this new bus service was not actually the first time one of the tentacles of London's transport system had reached Slough and Windsor. Almost 30 years previously, on 1st March 1883, the District line of the Underground system had started running through trains from the City to Windsor, using G.W.R. tracks. The idea was probably not a great success because the arrangement only lasted 2½ years but it shows how popular a destination Windsor was always perceived to be.

The 27th July edition of the Windsor Express reported that Eton Urban District Council had noted, without any apparent enthusiasm, that 'another bus service had now started running through the street' (the street obviously being Eton High Street). The councillors wondered whether seven daily waterings of the road surface were now enough to lay the dust; it was after all, high summer.

The cutting from 20th July edition of the Windsor paper on page 49 confirms the half hourly frequency at that stage and also its immediate, not to say instantaneous, popularity. No fewer than 4,357 passengers were carried, presumably both ways, on its first day which means that either each departure was run in triplicate or the frequency was immediately increased. The same paper reported the following under the Colnbrook News:

"Colnbrook in Touch with London by Road Cars - The enterprising London General Omnibus Company, seeing the possibility of opening up this somewhat neglected yet beautiful district, have started a new service of motor omnibuses which began running on Sundays only (at present) from Hounslow to Slough and Windsor, running along the Bath Road through Colnbrook. It became such an attraction that some 15 motor buses were kept on a continuous run backwards and forwards all day, and next Sunday the Company propose to put 30 buses on the route with an eight minutes' service. Colnbrook may yet see a revival of the old coaching times, when some 120 coaches, in touch with all the various towns and villages on and off the Bath Road, passed through per day between London and Bath and Bristol".

From the start, the General advertised inclusive single fares of one shilling from the City through to Windsor, but in practice, there was no through ticketing, then or later on.

Officially, the service became a daily one on Thursday, 1st August 1912, at which time it also changed its route number to 81. In practice, the expansion to a seven day a week facility may have happened a few days earlier because 27th July edition of the Windsor Express talked about the buses being less crowded on week days. That report, again under the Colnbrook news, was as follows; the reference to trams is interesting:

"The New Motor Bus Route - The London General Omnibus Co. have apparently done a very wise thing in putting on a daily service of motor buses between Hounslow and Windsor, for they appear to be greatly patronised by the general public, especially in those parts not in touch with the railway. On Sunday, as on previous occasions, the buses were crowded all day; some individuals made unsuccessful attempts to board the various buses passing, and had to be

content to walk home. On weekdays the buses are less crowded, the people only taking short journeys, so that there is a constant coming and going. Certainly the motor buses appear on the Bath Road to be better and handier than the tramcars and tramways, and the officials of the buses are already greatly in favour for their courtesy and attention to passengers".

34 - An L.G.O.C. bus parked outside the Horse & Groom in Windsor in July 1912 on the 62, later the 81, service.

The re-numbering of the service was part of a general move to re-number all the Underground feeder services in the 80's, the 84 from Golders Green tube station to St Albans being another example. The 81, which although finally cut back to Slough in 1963, has retained the same number for nearly 90 years, as has the 84 as a matter of fact.

The local papers were absolutely full of reports and comments on the new bus services; here are some extracts of what was being said:

Windsor Express - 27th July 1912

"London to Windsor - Tube and Omnibus Service Developed - The first great development in metropolitan and suburban transit following the combine between the District Railway, tubes and London General Omnibus Company will be achieved on Sunday next by the institution of a five-minute rail and motor omnibus service between the District Railway and Windsor. It is intended that this development shall be followed by the institution of a similar Sunday service to Burnham Beeches. The twelve-mile road service from Hounslow to Windsor is provided at the moderate rate of 6d.

In undertaking this important development the new combine has been guided entirely by the demand of the public. A fortnight ago a half-hourly service between Hounslow and Windsor was announced, but a fifteen-minute service was arranged as a provisional measure. So crowded were the omni- buses that on Sunday last a nine-minute service was instituted. This having proved insufficient to meet the demand, a regular five-minute service has been arranged. Thirty five buses and 55 drivers have now been licensed at Windsor."

Slough Chronicle - 2nd August 1912

"Railways versus Buses - The experiment of running motor buses between London and Windsor on Sundays has proved so successful that, as we foreshadowed, the London General Omnibus Company have converted the service into a daily one, and the appearance of these popular vehicles in the streets of the Royal borough are now almost as familiar as they are in places nearer the metropolis. Given a fine day there is no more delightful way of "taking the air", and though at present the journey to and from London is negotiated primarily as a pleasure trip the day cannot be far distant when people living in the Windsor, Eton and Slough districts will reach their businesses in town by motor bus in preference to the railway.

One good effect from the public point of view of this increased competition is that the railway companies will in all probability offer reduced fares to those taking return tickets. The present charge of 3 shillings for the journey to London and back is rightly regarded as excessive, and though on one afternoon a week sixpence is knocked off this sum, it is hardly worth consideration, as comparatively few Windsor people can travel on that day.

35 - An L.G.O.C. bus outside Hounslow underground station in July 1912, again on the 62 route.

The motor buses are conferring a great boon on people living in the villages along the route. Even where these places are served by the railways it is still quite a business to reach the nearest town, and where there are no trains the old-fashioned carrier has to be depended upon, with the result that a journey of a few miles can only be undertaken after some consideration, and then not more than once a week. But with the advent of the motor bus all this is changing, and what the railways, who have held the monopoly so long, have failed to do, the modern coach is accomplishing. It also allows the people to live under healthy conditions in the country while enabling them to reach the towns speedily and cheaply to make their purchases. The motor bus companies have been so occupied in capturing the traffic of the big towns that they have had no time to consider the possibilities of the villages, but now that they are doing so, the railways, like the trams, are beginning to feel the pinch, and if this leads to improved services the result will be beneficial all round".

Slough Chronicle - 9th August 1912

"1912 August Bank Holiday - There was one very marked difference to be noticed in Slough this year. Usually, on public holidays, the main thoroughfare of the town, except for motor traffic, bears a very deserted appearance, but on Monday one could barely look down High Street without sighting one of the now familiar motor buses proceeding either to Windsor or Hounslow, and there were very few which did not have their full complement of passengers. The introduction of this new service promises to make a considerable difference to Slough and prove a valuable connecting link with villages such as Colnbrook and Langley, the inhabitants of which greatly appreciate the additional facilities of getting to the nearest town".

Slough Chronicle - 16th August 1912

"In spite of the exodus of residents, however, the streets continue to present an animated appearance, thanks to the numerous parties of trippers who may be seen strolling about, and also to the motor buses which daily bring a

36 - The cover of the November 1912 General bus guide.

considerable number of visitors into the town. The cheapness of the fare from London is a great attraction, and many undertake the journey simply for the 'blow', returning without alighting, in the same bus in which they arrive. The success of their experiment has, we hear, led the London General Omnibus Company to consider the advisability of opening a garage in the district. As they now have about thirty-five vehicles on the route, with extensions to Burnham Beeches and Staines and others in contemplation, it is obvious that some central place for repairs, storage of petrol, etc is necessary. Suitable sites for a depot, either in Windsor or Slough, are, we understand, being considered, but nothing definite has yet been settled".

Slough Chronicle - 6th September 1912

"Editorial - In forming the waiting bus passengers at the top of Peascod Street, Windsor, into queues, the chief constable has hit upon an effective measure which has the advantage of being fair all round, as everybody gets a chance, and first to come are first served. In other towns there are sometimes miniature free fights round the vehicles, and chivalry is not encouraged, for the "mere man" who stands back to allow the ladies to step up, stands a very good chance of waiting for the next bus. There is, however, a good deal of obstruction still in the Windsor streets, especially on a Sunday evening. Peascod Street is, as a rule, filled with loiterers, and at the top of this thoroughfare a crowd of young people finds the fascination of watching the departure of the buses quite irresistible".

The reference to the possibility of building a local garage for the General buses in the Chronicle's 16th August extract is interesting, but nothing actually came to pass in this regard until long after the war. It was September 1926 before the General opened a garage in the area. It was sited at the junction of Langley Road and London Road, Langley and the building was only pulled down in 1999.

The increasing popularity of the 81 was reflected in an ever more frequent service. In August 1912, the weekday service was hourly from 9 o'clock in the morning until 8 o'clock at night, from the Hounslow end, and from 10.15 a.m. to 9.15 p.m. from the Windsor end. Since we know the journey took seventy minutes, the turn-around time at Windsor could only just have been long enough for the driver to enjoy a quick Woodbine before getting back into his open cab for the return journey. On Sundays, although the first departure was half an hour later, the frequency was every nine minutes. By September, the weekday frequency was every quarter of an hour and the Sunday frequency every seven minutes.

No sooner had the service become a daily one than it had to undergo a diversion through Eton as the High Street was closed for resurfacing during most of August. There had been no mention of this in the local Council report regarding laying the dust, but the resulting diversion might explain the mention of Keates Lane in a subsequent Council report which will crop up later because presumably the only possible alternative route was through that road and down to Meadow Lane before rejoining the High Street just before the river bridge.

Two of the above extracts referred to the planned start of a new service to Burnham Beeches and sure enough, on 18th August 1912, service 89 started running on Sundays only from The Bell at Hounslow (the 81 had already started using that as its terminus on every other journey) along the same route as the 81, that is to say, the old Bath Road, as far as Slough, Crown Corner. From there it continued along the Bath Road as far as Salt Hill, turning north to Farnham Royal. We should remember that what we now know as the Farnham Road was completely undeveloped, with fields on either side. Continuing up the main road to Farnham Common, it turned into Kingsway, along Hawthorn Lane, past The Stag and terminated at Wingroves Tea Rooms, as did the existing G.W.R. service. The through fare was 9d and the frequency was half-hourly; the first return journey from the Beeches was 11.35 a.m.

The fact that there were no early departures from the country end of these routes, obviously due to the lack of local garaging facilities, was probably not a major detraction from their popularity. Although the local paper had talked about commuters eventually choosing to go by bus to the City rather than use the train which was more expensive, it is very unlikely that this ever happened; nor I believe would a significant number of day trippers have gone to central London on the new services. The trade was almost certainly one way, as the newspaper reports referring to the social effects of the weekend invasions confirmed.

Reverting to the terminus of the Burnham Beeches service, it was Wingroves Tea Rooms which somehow or other endeared themselves to the bus operators in terms of mentions in timetables and even in official licences, although in fact they were only one of three such establishments. From the very outset, through to 1952, Wingroves was noted as the terminus for all the services although there were Macros Tea Rooms right opposite, on the corner of Hawthorn Lane and Lord Mayor's Drive (where the Estate offices currently are) and there was also the Brown Cow with its tea rooms and gardens on the same side of Hawthorn Lane as Wingroves. The T-junction with the bottom of Lord Mayor's Drive was obviously a practical point at which to turn round the buses and three point turns at

37 - An advertisement for Wingroves Tea Gardens taken from a 1912 or 1913 guide to Burnham Beeches.

that corner were the order of the day until the services eventually packed up. As can be seen from the advertisement taken from a 1912 or 1913 brochure on the Beeches, Wingroves were happy to acknowledge the L.G.O.C bus service although they did not mention the G.W.R. service which had been going for several years.

The service to the Beeches, which incidentally changed its number several times prior to the war as we shall see, was naturally destined for the leisure market as can be imagined and this is borne out by the fact it only ever operated on Sundays prior to the war; furthermore, it was withdrawn within five days of the outbreak of hostilities, that is to say on 9th August 1914. There was in fact however another reason why the service did not become a daily one up to the war, as we shall see in 1913.

The 6th September 1912 Slough Chronicle, apart from containing the report regarding queuing reproduced earlier, also mentioned two other items of note. The first was that the G.W.R. had apparently put on an additional through train from Paddington to Windsor on Sundays which the paper considered was 'doubtless as a result of the motor buses'. One train could of course carry the equivalent of a good many bus loads, but at three times the fare, it might not have been everybody's choice. The second item related to the licences which had been issued by Windsor Council to the General for the right for their services to ply for hire in the town. Thirty five buses had been licensed at five shillings a time (annual rate) and fifty five drivers at one shilling a time. This number of licences gave the General sufficient reserves for any foreseeable expansion of routes. The actual levies however, whilst being possibly at the top end of the scale compared with other local authorities, represented a miserly contribution towards the cost of road maintenance which was to become such an absolute *cause célèbre*.

Seeing nothing but good in the Sunday influx of potential shoppers at this stage, the Slough Observer in one of its September 1912 editions suggested that some form of shelter should be provided for the Londoners queuing to return home. To my knowledge, no such thing was ever done. Thinking about it, the Sunday restrictions on shop opening which prevailed in those days, and right up to fairly recently, meant that the only sort of businesses which were likely to benefit were catering establishments of every kind or leisure activities such as boating or river trips.

Before drawing 1912 to a close, it must be noted that during the latter part of that year and indeed right up to the outbreak of the war when more important matters came to the fore, there was an increasing undercurrent of criticism of motor bus operators nationally as well as locally regarding the fact they did not contribute to the increased costs of road maintenance caused by the regular passage of their heavy vehicles. It was pointed out in this debate that not only did the railways build their own 'roads' but in addition, they paid rates in respect of the areas covered by what we would today call their infrastructure. There were many column inches in the local papers on the topic and apparently in the national press as well. To give the flavour of the debate, there is reproduced as an Annexe on page 71 a typical article which actually appeared in the Slough Chronicle of 27th September 1912. It all contrasted rather ironically with the attitude taken in the early days of the G.W.R. services, noted in Chapter 3.

It would however be misleading to suggest that there was not on the other side, a great deal of favourable comment in the local papers regarding the convenience and commercial benefits of a cheap and frequent service of motor buses between Windsor and Slough. As an example of this side of the coin, the Slough Chronicle of 18th November 1912 reported that Windsor Council had decided not to send a delegate to a conference which had been called to discuss the whole question of motor buses and road maintenance. One councillor said that 'they did not want to do anything which might result in the curtailment of the splendid motor omnibus service which was doing so much for the town'.

A Parliamentary Commission was set up in 1914 to review the bus rateability question and after the war was over, the whole topic apparently reemerged. Eventually the anti-bus lobby lost the day and no form of levy was ever introduced.

The Burnham Beeches service was withdrawn some time between the October and November 1912 General leaflets and the frequency on the 81 was reduced on Sundays to the same 15 minute headway as on weekdays. These arrangements remained unchanged up to and including the April 1913 timetable.

38 - A G.W.R. bus en route to Burnham Beeches.

CHAPTER 8

During the first four months of 1913, there was no change in the pattern of motor bus services in the district; the G.W.R. continued to operate two services from Slough plus the Windsor to Ascot route and the General maintained a 15 minute frequency on their Hounslow to Slough and Windsor service. The latter was actually a very intensive schedule by local standards at that time, given that the G.W.R. services only averaged some eight to ten journeys a day.

There was a report in one of the February editions of the Slough Observer on the A.G.M. of the London General Omnibus Company. The company's fleet of motor buses had now reached almost 2,250 and during the latter half of 1912, they carried an average of 1.47 million passengers a day, the equivalent of 650 per bus. The average fare was only 1.3 old pence compared with 1.6 on the underground trains. The Chairman noted that the introduction of new routes such as the one to Windsor had diluted their profit margins. He concluded that "whilst admitting that it will take time for the new routes to become remunerative, it is doubtful if the earnings per individual motor bus will ever again equal those of previous years when the traffic was centred on the most remunerative routes only."

G.W.R. ROAD MOTORS.

The G.W.R. Company have made some important reductions in road motor car fares between Slough, Eton, and Windsor. It has long been possible to ride from Slough Station to the Prince of Wales for a penny, and now that humble coin will carry a passenger from the Crown Hotel to Barnespool Bridge, Eton, and from The Prince of Wales to Windsor G.W.R. Station. The fare from Slough Station is reduced to twopence, and by taking a return ticket on the motor car the passenger has the privilege of returning from Windsor by either road or rail whichever is convenient. Moreover, passengers by the railway will be able to return from Slough or Windsor by road motor with the return halves of their railway tickets. These arrangements ought to result in a great increase in the traffic between the two towns.

The details of the bill are as follows:
The fares by road motor will be as follows:

Between
Slough Station and the Prince of
  Wales ... ... Single 1d
The Crown and Barnespool Bridge „ 1d
Prince of Wales and Windsor
  Station ... ... „ 1d
Slough Station and Windsor Station „ 2d
  do.   do.   Return 4d

NOTE.—The return tickets will be available by either road motor or rail.
Return halves of rail tickets available between Slough and Windsor will also be available by either rail or road motor car.

39 - Report in 4th January 1913 edition of the Slough Observer on the reduction in the G.W.R. bus fares, caused undoubtedly by L.G.O.C. competition; the rail and bus return tickets also became inter-changeable

The 3rd May edition of the Slough Observer noted without any further explanation that the General would commence running to Maidenhead at Whitsun; they were right. On the 11th of the month, a new service, numbered 110, was started on Sundays only from Hounslow Barracks Station to that town. Its route coming out from Hounslow was the same as the 81 as far as the beginning of London Road, Langley; from there, it turned down Ditton Road into Datchet High Street. This was the first motor bus service to Datchet although there had certainly been horse-bus services. As long ago as some 60 years previously, there had been such a service from there to Windsor via Eton, prior to the final extension of the London and South Western Railway's line to Windsor Riverside station.

The day before the motor bus service started, the Slough Observer carried the following report of a meeting of the Eton Urban District Council which discussed the new route amongst other things:

"The London General Omnibus Company applied for licences for 32 motor omnibuses and 52 drivers' licences. It was stated that the company intended to open a new route between Windsor and Maidenhead via Eton on Whit-Sunday and Whit-Monday, and if the conditions were favourable application would be made for a renewal of the licences at the end of the month.

The Chairman said they could not keep the buses out; if they refused the licences the only results would be that the buses would not be able to take up and set down passengers in their district.

It was decided to grant the licences, and at the same time point out to the company that if they proposed to use Keates Lane the council anticipated considerable danger owing to the bad corners."

Continuing the route of the 110, it approached Windsor through the Home Park and turned up into Thames Street (no one way system in those days), past the Castle and the Guildhall to the far end of the High Street; from there it used Sheet Street and Victoria Street to reach Clarence Road before turning down Vansittart Road and out along the Maidenhead Road. It went through Braywick and into Maidenhead, terminating at the river bridge. The fare for the whole journey from Hounslow which took an hour and 50 minutes (we must remember that the maximum permitted speed was only 12 miles an hour), was 10 old pence, say 4 new pence.

On the same day as the service 110 started, that is to say 11th May 1913, the Hounslow to Burnham Beeches service was re-introduced for the summer season; this time, it was numbered 112 and operated via Stoke Poges when proceeding between Slough and Farnham Royal instead of via Salt Hill as previously; Stoke Poges church had visitor potential whereas what we now call the Farnham Road was devoid of any tourist attractions, as indeed it is today!

The new Maidenhead service represented a significant advance for that town in terms of outside road links; there had only been some modest local motor bus routes operated by the G.W.R. up to that time and the company which was to service the town and its surroundings for the next 50 years, namely the Thames Valley Traction Company, only made its first appearance, reaching Maidenhead from Reading, in July 1915. The traffic potential of a direct road link from Windsor to Maidenhead which could only be travelled indirectly by rail by changing at Slough, as is still the case today, was not lost on the General. Within 8 days of starting the Sunday service, a weekday service was introduced between Windsor Castle and Maidenhead, a 45 minute journey at that time. It is surprising that there had been no such motorised link up until then, bearing in mind there had even been an abortive light railway proposal to connect the two towns as far back as 1901. Apparently, the small number of buses required to operate the new route ran in service on the 81 from Hounslow morning and evening.

At the risk of boring my readers, it has to be repeated that the papers continued to be absolutely obsessed by the question of the bus companies getting away scot free whilst tearing up the inadequate road surfaces which, in many cases, had only just been laid. The following letter, by way of further example, appeared in 31st May 1913 edition of the Slough Observer:

"Sir - "A Victim" says that it seems a pity that the Slough Council opposed the trams coming to Slough. No doubt it is a pity. The trams, like the Great Western Railway, would have paid large sums in rates, and the motor buses are paying no rates. "A Victim" suggests that the council should try their utmost to get some rates out of the motor buses. Well, if the council cannot rate the motor buses they ought to be able to get some money in lieu of rates out of them. The buses have to obtain licences from the council, and surely they can require some payment in lieu of rates before they grant those licences. We know that the buses have to pay half the petrol tax, but that money is hoarded by the Road Board for improvements and is not available for road maintenance. We want some money to keep up the roads for the buses, and the council ought to make some attempt to get it. If they cannot get it from the Road Board, they should try the bus proprietors. Yours faithfully, EQUITY."

It is quite clear that Slough Urban District Council were being singularly unsuccessful in extracting significant sums of money from the General. In a long report on one of the council debates during the first half of June on the potential rateability of buses, which noted that there are 'nearly a 100 on our roads', it was stated that only £31.5.6d (£31.27½) had been collected for drivers' licences and £600 for bus licences. Some of the councillors were clearly still sensitive about the trams fiasco 9 years previously, pointing out that the outcome 'was not their fault, all the differences with the tramway company having been resolved'! On the road maintenance topic, the Council decided quite categorically in July that bus operators **should** pay towards road upkeep but in the absence of legislation, they could think of no way to enforce such a contribution.

Meanwhile, not all the citizens of Datchet were thrilled by their new Sunday bus service. One of them apparently wrote in June to the Morning Post, a national newspaper, along the following lines:

"Mr Lloyd George recently apologised for making a speech in Wales on a Sunday. It is comforting to think that there is one part of the United Kingdom where Sunday is still held in respect and one Minister of the Crown who is not afraid to speak of the sacredness of Sunday.

In England, especially in the vicinity of London, Sunday is rapidly ceasing to be either a sacred day or even a day of rest. The advent of the motor bus is altering the habits of the people, and at the same time doing grievous harm to the amenities of the countryside.

It would be churlish to resent the idea of the Londoners' wish to escape from the heated streets to the green lanes of the country. For many, Sunday is the only day available for this purpose, and one would not wish to grudge anyone this enjoyment. It is not the fact of the motor bus service, but the methods, which cause annoyance, amounting almost to bitter execration, in the country round London throughout a Sunday during the summer season.

On a Sunday morning several motor buses during the hour pass round Datchet parish church and stop on the green. The disturbance to the church services, the general atmosphere of a suburban railway station thus produced, are by no means peculiar to the village in question.

> The Great Western Railway road motor omnibus between Slough and Windsor has now been withdrawn over a week, and it is very much missed, especially by the inhabitants at the London end of Slough, who found it a great convenience in getting from Slough Station to their dwellings. We don't know whether it would be possible for the London General Omnibus Company to run their Slough and Maidenhead buses via Wellington-street and Wexham-road and so supply the place of the G.W.R. bus. If they could do so, it would be an additional convenience if they could connect them with the fast trains which arrive at Slough. Many passengers could then get out of the trains into the buses and be conveyed almost to their own doors.

40 - Report in 9th August 1913 edition of the Slough Observer on the replacement of the G.W.R. service by the L.G.O.C; the plea to synchronise bus and train timings was an early demand for integrated transport, still being sought after these days!

Private houses abutting on the green or the roads down which the new Sunday traffic passes in this interminable stream have no longer any privacy or repose during Sunday, and their value as property is sensibly diminished.

A further accentuation of the annoyance is caused by the motor buses being covered with advertisements of soap, whiskey, and the like, and of the performances at the leading London theatres.

It is possible to tolerate the motor buses on the ground of the pleasure they give to those who use them. It is quite possible also for the omnibus company to organise their services to be of real benefit to the countryside, instead of mere cartage of cockney trippers. There can however be no excuse for filling the country lanes and village greens with a cinema show of moving advertisements, especially on Sunday".

In July 1913, some sort of agreement was apparently made between the G.W.R. and the General. In return for the General agreeing not to turn their Sundays-only service to Burnham Beeches into a full 7-day operation, the G.W.R. agreed to withdraw their Slough-Windsor route (naturally, they still had the train service between those two towns), thus leaving the General as the sole operator on that busy corridor.

To fill the gap, the General extended their weekday Maidenhead to Windsor service back to Slough station, via Eton High Street, Windsor Road (Slough) and Mackenzie Street. This took place on 24th July, the G.W.R. service being terminated within 2 days. In spite of its deviation from the original route, these Maidenhead/Slough journeys were also numbered 110; the frequency was still half-hourly as it had been when the service terminated in Windsor.

41 - A G.W.R. bus in familiar surroundings, almost certainly on a race day.

Again, the positioning journeys from Hounslow to the nearest starting point, now Slough station, ran in service morning and evening but the change meant that Datchet was now back to only enjoying a road link on Sundays. Even that was to disappear in October; Sunday the 19th was the last day that year the service came out from London and the following Sunday, the weekday service from Slough station to Maidenhead was made into a daily facility. So Datchet was to have to wait until May 1914 before the dreaded advertisements on wheels would once again desecrate its pleasant green.

The result of these changes was that the G.W.R. had been transformed within 15 months from being the only motor bus operator in the district to being a minor player with only two services. The General now dominated the scene as indeed their successor, London Transport, would continue to do until bus privatisation in 1986.

The Maidenhead Advertiser in one of its August 1913 editions enthused over 'the fine new bus service' and at the end of that month carried a graphic report of an aeroplane just skimming over the top of a General bus before crashing into a field near Bray cemetery. The bus en route from Windsor to Maidenhead, had 'a fair number of passengers on board' and those on the top deck were (not surprisingly!) 'very interested' The driver of the bus was the first man on the scene.

In the same month, Slough council became quite agitated by the fact that without so much as by your leave, the General had sent out one of its tree lopping buses to cut the trees in the Windsor Road. The Chairman of the Council said: "I think it is a good cheek to come down here and cut our trees" and the Surveyor went on to say "In my opinion, the trees have been mutilated." In spite of having received a written apology from the L.G.O.C., the general mood of the meeting was quite critical of motor bus operators and the Chairman concluded by saying "They will take the earth soon"! So feelings about the new bus services were not all favourable by any means. As a matter of fact, tree cutting became a subject of regular correspondence between the General and the

REDHILL AND THE MOTOR BUSES.

Reigate Town Council refused on Tuesday to confirm the action of the Watch Committee in granting 25 licences to the London General Omnibus Company to ply for hire in Redhill. The company has organised a Sunday service of busses between Stockwell and Redhill.

Mr. Perren said the buses brought down a lot of the riff-raff, and Alderman Malcomson complained of the singing of rowdy songs.

Mr. Ince stated that the Watch Committee were unanimous against the granting of the licences, but after taking advice they found it would be futile to refuse them.

It was pointed out by the Town Clerk that, although the council had discretionary powers, they had to exercise their discretion in a reasonable and just manner.

Alderman Malcomson replied that the licences should still be refused. If they were compelled to grant the licences they could climb down.

42 - Redhill objected to the riff-raff the L.G.O.C. buses brought in (Slough Observer, 23rd August 1913).

local councils; the height of the double deckers with their vulnerable passengers on top, was something for which there had not been much precedent.

Two items came up in the Windsor paper in the Autumn of 1913 relating to the potential risk of road accidents resulting from the new giant motor omnibuses. The first pointed out, no doubt prompted by remarks originally made by the Chief Constable at High Wycombe, that the risk of accidents would be much reduced if the buses could be required to stop only at recognised stopping places; in fact this did not happen even in London until the late 1920's. The second was in October when there was a report of a boy being killed by a bus whilst cycling over Windsor bridge. This subject quickly developed into more criticism of the bus operators not being required to pay anything towards road improvements, in this case the widening of the bridge to take the buses; it was pointed out that a tramway company would have had to pay for widening.

To conclude 1913, on 18th October, the Sundays only route to Burnham Beeches, numbered 112, went into its winter hibernation, to reappear in 1914 under a new number.

And so we move into 1914, a year seen in retrospect by many as the peak of our civilisation. As a matter of interest, the local papers in Slough and Windsor were devoid of any thought of an impending war with Germany, right up to the day it broke out; they were far more preoccupied with 'the Irish question'.

To come back to our subject, we should just recapitulate the motor bus services which were operating during the winter of 1913/14. The G.W.R. maintained their daily service from Slough station to Farnham Common (Hedgerley Corner) via Stoke Green, the summer journeys to Burnham Beeches having also gone into winter hiding, plus their Windsor to Ascot route. The General were also running two daily services, the 81 from Hounslow (the new garage there opened in December 1913) to Slough and Windsor and the 110 starting at Slough and going through Windsor to Maidenhead. So far as I know, none of these services deviated from the main roads, to serve Chalvey for example, or any other isolated pockets of population. The two General routes between them provided no less than 6 journeys an hour between our two towns and of course the railway service continued to operate although that was no good for intending Eton travellers. At what point the horse-bus service decided to call it a day is not known.

There were no changes to these services until May 1914 when, as we shall see, there was a quite bewildering number of alterations. Meanwhile, the annual report on the financial affairs of the General appeared in February, as it had the previous year. The number of passengers carried on the buses in 1913 had increased by some 30% compared with 1912, to an impressive total of 1.9 million. All these travellers had generated substantial profits and resulting dividends (18%): furthermore, the company which manufactured and maintained all the new buses for the General (Associated Equipment Company - 'AEC') was actually paying a dividend of 34%. All this provoked further calls for rates to be paid by the General and it was these and other demands across the whole country which finally led to the House of Commons setting up the new Commission already referred to. As previously mentioned, nothing ever came of all these objections.

One fascinating statistic was quoted in the Slough Observer in March; apparently, no fewer than 1,374 people had been killed on the roads in 1913. This meant that almost four road users lost their lives each day which is approximately a third of the number of fatalities we suffer today. It shows how incredibly unmindful the population must have been of the potential dangers of the new and relatively fast motorised vehicles, given that there were still only 207,000 such vehicles on the road at that time, or three quarters of 1% of today's total. Apparently, falling off bus platforms was quite a high contributor to the problem and a letter to the London Evening Standard suggested that there should be communication cords on buses as there were on trains.

Before reverting to the London General services, the G.W.R. introduced one modest expansion in our area before the war came along to curtail their operations. The 28th March 1914 edition of the Slough Observer carried an advertisement (reproduced on this page) announcing a new road motor car service between Burnham and Hurley via Maidenhead station, to operate on weekdays and Sundays 'at convenient intervals'. Between Burnham and Maidenhead there were to be stops at Lent Rise Cross Roads, Taplow station and Maidenhead River station (I understand this used to be up on the embankment opposite the Dumb Bell pub); I do not believe that the fact these stops were specified meant that the buses would not stop almost anywhere else on request.

The Burnham end was obviously not popular on Sundays (the Hurley end had a golf course) because by 4th April, the Sunday service was restricted to the westerly end of the route. Regardless of that, this was the first motor bus service to reach Burnham and it apparently started from the Crispin pub at the top of the High Street (the name of the pub was inexplicably changed to the Bee in February 1999). Within four weeks of the service starting, Burnham Parish Council was recommending the G.W.R. should reduce the fare from the Crispin to Maidenhead from one shilling to 8 old pence. Even at this level, it was expensive by London General standards. These high fares were still worrying the same

> **G. W. R.**
>
> **New Road Motor Car Service**
> BETWEEN
> **Maidenhead Station and Hurley and Burnham,**
>
> COMMENCING APRIL 1st, 1914.
>
> WEEK DAY AND SUNDAY CARS in both directions at convenient intervals.
>
> Intermediate stops to set down and pick up passengers will be made at the "Windsor Castle," Thicket Corner, Camley Corner (for Pinkney's Green), Coach and Horses, Littlewick Green, Burchetts Green, Temple Golf Club, Maidenhead River Station, Taplow Station, and Lent Rise Cross Roads.
> For full details see bills.
>
> FRANK POTTER, General Manager.

43 - Advertisement for new G.W.R. service which appeared in 28th March 1914 edition of the Slough Observer.

council as late as June; one councillor said that 'the present G.W.R. service was only a convenience for the driver and conductor as there were scarcely any passengers due to excessive fares'. The council went on to ask the up and coming L.G.O.C. to run from the village to Maidenhead so as to connect with their buses from there to Windsor and Slough; that may seem a long way round to get to Slough but there was no direct motorised link by road between Slough and Burnham at that stage.

May 1914 was the month in which the seasonal burgeoning of London General services took place. On the 3rd of the month, route 110 was extended north from Slough station up the Stoke Poges road, through the Farnhams and into Burnham Beeches (once again Wingroves Tea Rooms to be precise). There was a bus every 15 minutes. Since there was, as just noted, still no motorised link between Slough and Burnham village and only the overpriced service between there and Maidenhead, one would have thought that completing this link and making a circular route of it would have made a lot of sense. Admittedly, the extension to the Beeches did only operate on Sundays and in fact it only ran for four Sundays before being replaced by a new route.

From 14th May to 27th July, the road bridge linking Eton and Windsor was closed to traffic for maintenance purposes. To accommodate this, the 81 was terminated at the bridge and the 110 was re-routed between Slough and Windsor via Albert Street, Slough, Datchet Road, Datchet itself, over the Victoria Bridge and through the Home Park.

On Sunday 31st May 1914, three new, or to be more precise, three replacement Sunday services were introduced by the London General as follows:

Route 175   Hounslow to Burnham Beeches, which replaced the previous year's service 112.

Route 177   Eton to Burnham Beeches, which replaced the Sunday extension of the 110 from Slough to the Beeches, but extended back at the other end to Eton.

Route 179   Hounslow to Maidenhead, replacing the previous year's 110 Sunday service, again via Datchet and Windsor, by-passing Slough.

The 175 was a 94 minute journey at a slightly inflated fare of 9½d (say 4 new pence) and the 110 minute journey to Maidenhead on the 179 now cost 11d. The 177 service, which like the other two operated half-hourly, cost 5d. for a 44 minute ride. It had one very intriguing characteristic noted in the monthly timetable leaflet at the time; this was that it only operated 'if fine'. Was it the responsibility of the inspector on duty at Eton to decide whether that criterion had been met - hopefully, he did not disappoint too many Etonians heading for the great outdoors! More interestingly perhaps was from whence could he rustle up a bus to fulfill the promise; maybe he had to commandeer a passing 81. All this is probably rather fanciful; the decision was almost certainly taken in far away Hounslow.

Talking of the 81, the weekday frequency in the summer of 1914 was only half-hourly compared with every 15 minutes the previous year and the fare had gone up by a 1d.

The reason why the route numbers of these services had shot up since 1913 was that the General had incorporated the ex-National Steam Car Company services into their numbering system at the start of 1914 and had also introduced a number of new services of their own in the intervening months. When the seasonal services re-started in the summer of 1914, they had to take their new place in the pecking order.

At the end of July, the G.W.R. reduced their fares on their Burnham Beeches service by 25% in response to the competition from the General; Slough station to Stoke Poges cross-roads was now only 3d, to Farnham Royal 4d and to Wingroves, 6d. Talking of that establishment, the volume of customers for them and hopefully for the other cafes in the Beeches must have been quite phenomenal in the three summers up to the outbreak of the war, bearing in mind that virtually nobody would have come by car in previous years.

And so on 4th August 1914, this country went to war with Germany. The effect on the bus operations we have been considering was almost immediate. The Eton to Burnham Beeches service had prophetically terminated the day before and the other two Sunday services were withdrawn on 9th August. The 110 from Slough to Maidenhead lasted until 7th November 1914 and the 81 finally stopped on 30th January 1915; the latter was actually restarted for a short period during the war.

These withdrawals were not due to petrol rationing which was to only come in in 1917, but because the Army commandeered a large number of the General's vehicles with immediate effect. By the end of the very day war was declared, some 700 London buses had been taken off the roads. At the peak, the Army took over 40% of the General's fleet, most of which were shipped overseas. Even the horses were commandeered, thus finally bringing to an end this mode of bus traction on the streets of the capital.

44 - The caption says it all - L.G.O.C. bus in May 1914.

By way of local illustration of the problems now facing the General, the members of Eton Urban District Council were told at their September meeting that the bus company had written to them saying that the War Office had commandeered 34 out of the 90 buses Eton had only just licensed in June and could they please have another 34 to replace them; doubtless, in the spirit of the time, the Council decided that 'this was a very fair proposal.'

Two further local reports, which appeared in October, illustrated the state of war which now existed. The first was that no fewer than 80 ex London General double deckers had been seen passing westwards through Slough one Saturday evening with two soldiers in each; I find this quite a chilling image. They were presumably heading eventually for one of the Channel ports, to be taken over to Flanders with the many others that ended their days there. The second report stated that the continuous stream of heavy War Office vehicles had completely worn off the coating of tar which had been only recently applied to Slough High Street, making the dust 'intolerable'. This was clearly a continuing problem!

Meanwhile the G.W.R. had fared much better than the General, probably because their fleet was not standardised and was possibly less reliable than the General's B-type double deckers. The railway company's service to Burnham Beeches finished at the end of September 1914 which was the end of the season in any case and surprisingly, the South Bucks tour also went on until then. The non-seasonal services from Slough to Farnham Common (Hedgerley Corner) and from Windsor to Ascot continued throughout the War, partially due presumably to the fact that there was no alternative rail service between those places. The struggling Burnham to Maidenhead service finished at the beginning of December 1914 and as previously noted, the Stoke Park service came to an end in July 1915.

Thus our story has reached its conclusion. The motor bus had come a long way in the eleven years covered by this book and so far as Slough, Windsor and the surrounding area was concerned, its image had changed from one of being an unquestioningly welcome thing to that of being a bit of a mixed blessing. With the motor car still virtually absent from the scene, the bus had undoubtedly transformed the daily lives of the general populace, particularly those who lived on the edge of or outside the towns. Some local businesses had thrived as never before and the local Councils' road maintenance budget had been multiplied several times over. Perhaps the influx of day trippers from London had changed the way the resident population looked at the area they were living in and reminded them of how fortunate they were to be so near such lovely country; so near and yet so far, unless they happened to live on one of the still limited number of bus routes.

The increase in services during the last three years of our period was as nothing compared with what would happen after the war. The General would return in force and there would also be an increase in one-man bus operators. Young men would come back from Army service having acquired free of charge a knowledge of how to drive and maintain a motorised vehicle. The existence of the War Office vehicle dump on their doorstep at

Slough would give them local access to newly refurbished commercial chassis at knock-down prices. Free of today's restrictions on safety, they could build themselves a makeshift body which might be so austere that it served as a goods van overnight, to stock up at the London markets, and as a bus during the day time. The Windsor/Slough corridor became a race track for some 30 or 40 one-man bus operators, all in desperate and unfettered competition.

But all that will be another story ....

ANNEXE

(Extracts from article taken from 27th September 1912 edition of the Slough Chronicle)

MOTOR OMNIBUSES : SHOULD THEY BE TAXED?

THE LOCAL COUNCILS AND ROAD REPAIRS - The question of the rival merits of the motor omnibuses and the trams as public conveyances is attracting considerable attention just now, and it would appear from the publication of the result of the working of the two systems that the buses are gradually ousting the trams from the roads. During the past six months there was a fall in passenger receipts on the seven tramway systems of London of £64,000. Against this decline is an increased earning by the London General Omnibus Company of £514,000 in eleven months. This is a serious matter to those boroughs which have municipalised their tramway system, and on the face of it it is a proof that private enterprise can do better than municipal trading. But in considering the question it has to be remembered that while the tramways contribute largely to the upkeep of the roads, the omnibuses pay nothing, and it is alleged against them that they do infinitely more damage. The question of buses v trams, which bulks so largely in the London papers, is not one that directly concerns the ratepayers of the Windsor neighbourhood as the district is not served by the latter, but with the advent of the motor buses it is certainly the duty of the local authorities for Windsor, Eton and Slough to consider whether they ought not to combine with other councils in an effort to obtain substantial contributions from motor omnibus companies for the use of the roads.

THE WINDSOR DISTRICT - In the case of the Windsor district it is perhaps too early yet to say what damage, if any, has been done to the roads, though the Eton Rural District Council seems to have made up its mind on this point. During the recent closing of Eton High Street for repairs, vehicular traffic was diverted to the roads controlled by the Rural District Council, which is now calling upon the Urban District Council of Eton for a contribution towards the upkeep, and threatens legal proceedings if it is not forthcoming.

INCREASED COST OF ROADS - From all the country comes the cry that the increased cost of the roads due to motor traffic is largely responsible for the burdens placed upon the ratepayers. At Kingston-on-Thames it is estimated that a twenty-minute service of motor omnibuses has increased the cost of the upkeep of the roads by one-third. At Surbiton it is estimated that over £200 damage has been done to the roads by motor omnibuses, which started running six months ago. At Willesden £6,000 has been spent in three years in paving roads with wood to fit them for motor omnibus traffic. During the five years motor omnibuses have been running at Barnes, £37,000 has been spent in substituting wood paving for the ordinary surface.

Thirty five motor buses have been licensed in Windsor, and these provided, roughly speaking, a quarter of an hour service during the week, which is increased to practically a five minute service on Sunday. If it is found that the damage done to local roads compares in any degree with the amount estimated by other local bodies, then the small licensing fee of 5s. per bus (which is at present paid) will hardly compensate the ratepayers.

MOTOR BUS BENEFITS - It is argued in favour of the buses that they bring a large number of visitors into the district; this is undeniable, and to places such as Windsor, which are rather indifferently served by the railway companies, they have undoubtedly proved a great boon. It is also contended by supporters of the motor bus that it has actually led to numerous thoroughfares being improved out of all recognition, at the same time effecting a great saving to the ratepayers.

BEST FORM OF ROAD - On the other hand, Colonel Crompton, the consulting engineer to the Road Board, expressed the opinion that macadam bonded with tar or some other form of bituminous binder is cheaper than wood for heavy traffic. It is interesting to note on the question of maintenance that the taxation yield from motor cars, cabs, and omnibuses and commercial vehicles is already in a typical London street, such as Piccadilly, more than enough by several hundred pounds per mile per annum to pay the cost of maintenance. But it is a grievance with many local authorities that the petrol tax yield is not available for direct application on the roads concerned, but only to improvements, and so far no borough in any part of the country has been able to get a grant from the Road Board.

APPORTIONING THE WEAR AND TEAR - At present only a short stretch of road is used by the buses in the borough of Windsor, and this will make it easier to apportion the wear and tear due to increased traffic. But it is contemplated to considerably extend the present route, with the result that more roads in the borough will be travelled over, and, as each wheel of a motor bus is stated to produce a pressure of from four to seven tons, according to the speed at which the vehicle is going, it is quite obvious that the surface of the road must suffer. To withstand such pressure requires a road of wood, asphalt or macadam with a 22inch foundation. Are any roads in the neighbourhood so constructed?

DAMAGE TO HOUSE PROPERTY - Complaints are being made by residents and property owners in narrow thoroughfares through which motor buses pass, that their houses are being shaken to the foundations, and it is not at all unlikely that in the congested streets like Eton High Street, complaints of a similar nature will be received. At present the companies can use any street, whether it is adapted for motor bus traffic or not.

A TAX SUGGESTION - The whole question of road maintenance requires very serious consideration. A number of local authorities have become so alarmed at the ravages caused by motor traffic that they are agitating for a clause to be introduced into next year's Finance Act, giving the proceeds of the petrol tax or other charges on motor omnibuses to local authorities in proportion to the use made of the roads in the various areas. We hope that the matter will not escape the attention of local councillors, as any further expenditure on the roads out of the ratepayers pockets would be strongly resented.